1985 Porsche 911 Turbo.

911 HUL

PORSCHE PROGRESS

Stuttgart's modern development story

PORSCHE PROGRESS

Stuttgart's modern development story

Michael Cotton

Patrick Stephens Limited
Wellingborough, Northamptonshire

© Michael Cotton/1988

First published in 1988

British Library Cataloguing in Publication Data

Cotton, Michael, 1938-
PORSCHE PROGRESS
Stuttgart's modern development story
1. Porsche automobile—History
I. Title
629.2'222   TL215.P75

ISBN 0-85059-928-8

Patrick Stephens is part of the
Thorsons Publishing Group,
Wellingborough, Northamptonshire,
NN8 2RQ, England

Printed in Great Britain by
The Bath Press, Bath, Avon

1 3 5 7 9 10 8 6 4 2

Contents

Acknowledgements

Directors of a company such as Porsche have many claims on their time, and work longer hours than those who serve them. In the preparation of this book I was deeply impressed by the willingness of Peter Schutz, Professor Bott and Dipl Ing Paul Hensler to be interviewed at length, with a tape recorder running, and with never a glance at their wristwatches. They enabled me to prepare what might be called a semi-official record of the company's growth, successes, and a few setbacks since 1975, an era which has seen profound changes in management philosophy, model line-up, manufacturing techniques, and in competitions too.

Thanks are due to Jeremy Snook of Porsche Cars Great Britain and the staff of the Presseabteilung in Zuffenhausen, in particular to Klaus Reichert, Begoña Gosch, and Klaus Parr for allowing me full access to the archives.

Assistance with background information was freely given by Jerry Sloniger and by Lars-Roger Schmidt, and I thank them too.

A modern history is necessarily vulnerable to fresh events, and this is no exception. In December 1987 Peter Schutz's tenure as chief executive ended prematurely, by a few months, by mutual agreement with the company's supervisory board. This in no way alters the tenor of the book, nor does it detract from the enormous expansion and modernisation that has taken place in the period 1974-1987. As it turns out, Porsche Progress is a monument both to Professor Fuhrmann and to Peter Schutz. With hindsight, I would have written it no differently.

Foreword

Michael Cotton has succeeded in capturing the most interesting developments of modern Porsche history. The period of the company's growth that is described, traces the adolescence; a most interesting and stormy period in the development of a company, just as it is in a human being. It is a period rich in youthful excitement, with the many painful learning experiences so typical to this period in a life-cycle.

The book clearly leaves one 'wanting more'. It was in fact Professor Porsche who responded to a reporter's question: 'What is your favourite Porsche of all time?' with: 'We haven't built it yet!'

I was left with the distinct impression that 'the best is yet to come'.

Peter W. Schutz

Introduction

As automotive manufacturers go, Dr Ing hc F Porsche AG, in Stuttgart-Zuffenhausen and Weissach, is in a minor league. Between 1948 and the end of 1986, the company produced about 660,000 cars, and production is currently running at a rate of little more than 50,000 cars per annum. At the other end of the spectrum, General Motors makes that many every couple of days, yet Porsche's influence in the world, and the excitement caused by its products, is out of all proportion to its size.

The product lines, though outwardly changing little each year, are continually improved. The realms of performance are climbing steadily, always coupled with improvements in fuel consumption, dynamics and acoustics. Traditionally half the Porsches made are sold in America and yet, despite the overall 65 mph (110 km/h) speed limit in that great continent, Porsche's management has discovered that any attempt to limit the car's performance, perhaps in the interests of better engine flexibility or improved fuel economy, has been resisted in the market place.

At least ten per cent of Porsche's turnover, and far more of its prestige value, lies in the research and development centre at Weissach. Many of the world's 130 recognized manufacturers have specialized development work carried out in secrecy at this Mecca of engineering research, and some such as Lada and Seat have engines, transmissions or entire family cars developed there on the fringe of the Black Forest.

Until 1974, Porsche held the main development contracts for Volkswagen, a carry-over from pre-war times when founder Professor Ferdinand Porsche designed the 'people's car' that came to be known as the 'Beetle'. The loss of that contract, coupled with the first oil crisis, was a body-blow to the small Porsche company as demand for its own products, centred on the six-cylinder 911 range, fell below the critical 10,000 mark in a year.

Everything that Porsche has done—and that includes investments exceeding DM1,000 million in new plant and facilities in the 1980s—has been with Porsche's own money, from reserve funds. Reliance upon the American market, always central to Porsche's product philosophy, can be a two-edged sword; in good times dollar profits pay for enormous expansion, but when the DM/$ relationship is poor it is time to batten down the hatches.

Professor Ferdinand 'Ferry' Porsche.

Peter W Schutz, chief executive at Porsche from 1981 to 1987.

Peter W. Schutz, appointed chief executive in January 1981, is a German-born American who applied new philosophies and a better understanding of the American way of life. Under his stewardship, production virtually doubled and so did the number of employees. Turnover tripled while profits rose tenfold. Peter Schutz's contract was terminated in December 1987 and his successor is Heinz Branitzki, former finance director and deputy chairman since 1976.

It is logical to start this book in 1975, a year in which some decisions very crucial to the future of the company had to be made, and massive investment allocated to the launch of the 924 model at a time of vanishing profits. The course was then set to turn Porsche into a company with not one but three main model lines, with opportunities to widen and strengthen its dealer network. No longer would Porsche be reliant upon the 911, which might have been phased out of production in 1984 had Professor Dr Fuhrmann's plan been adhered to. Ironically that model is in greater demand than ever. As an extension of the 911 policy the futuristic 959 model has, rather belatedly, been produced and delivered to 200 wealthy customers, and its technological features are now being studied for integration into the model range.

This is a success story, though it starts and ends at a critical period in Porsche's history, and encompasses another crisis in 1980/81 and 1987/88, which Porsche was by no means alone in enduring. The tabulated data shows graphically how

Porsche's volume production, exports, labour force, turnover, investments and profits have fared in this period, a company health-check in other words, and helps to explain the raison d'être for this book.

In this time, too, Porsche has enjoyed some outstanding successes in sports car racing using production-derived six-cylinder engines with 10 Le Mans victories in the period 1976 to 1987, and has been contracted by TAG to design, build, develop and maintain Formula 1 engines which have won World Championships in 1984, 1985 and 1986. These are not, in fact, central to this book, though they constantly add prestige to Porsche's research centre at Weissach.

Dr Ing hc F Porsche AG Progress 1972 to 1987

Financial Year (to July)	Production volume	Exports per cent	US sales	Employees	Turnover DM millions	Investments DM millions	Profits DM millions
1972-73	14,678	73	6,025	4,077	425.5	25.3	7.5
1973-74	11,793	78	5,572	3,731	397.0	25.4	0.1
1974-75	8,618	74	4,732	3,386	353.2	139.5	2.4
1975-76	20,637	66	9,093	3,713	604.3	47.9	7.5
1976-77	37,435	74	20,757	4,316	1,002.5	72.6	17.0
1977-78	35,187	69	17,348	4,849	1,123.2	57.0	10.0
1978-79	41,350	65	16,804	5,031	1,350.1	57.2	22.8
1979-80	31,138	66	11,844	4,948	1,234.7	55.7	10.0
1980-81	28,015	66	7,796	4,906	1,165.2	80.5	10.0
1981-82	32,640	68	11,482	5,273	1,488.2	125.7	37.6
1982-83	45,240	73	20,235	5,883	2,133.7	131.1	69.6
1983-84	44,773	72	20,647	6,512	2,494.3	254.5	92.4
1984-85	50,514	75	24,880	7,915	3,175.7	290.8	120.4
1985-86	53,625	79	28,671	8,458	3,567.9	272.2	75.3
1986-87	50,715	84	30,718	8,556	3,408.6	272.3	N/A

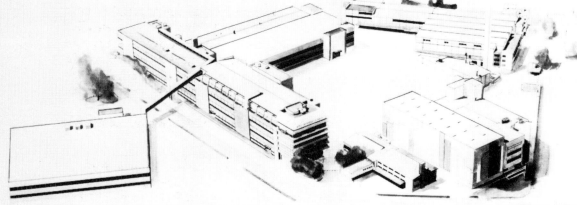

1

From the recession

The story of Porsche's development in terms of products and company growth logically begins in 1975 when the 924 model was announced, involving the Stuttgart-Zuffenhausen firm in buy-out, development and launch costs that could scarcely be afforded as demand for the 911 model was in a trough. But to understand what decisions were made at that time we need to go back to 1971, when major changes were taking place.

Until 1974, Dr Ing hc F Porsche AG held a major, but exclusive development contract with Volkswagen. Some 100 engineers who moved from Zuffenhausen to the new Weissach facility in 1971 under the direction of Dipl Ing Ferdinand Piëch, were busily involved in designing and developing a successor to the Beetle, another rear-engined model code-named (in VW's system) EA 266. Several prototypes were up and running in 1971 with overhead camshaft four-cylinder engines, water-cooled, laid flat beneath the rear seats, and privately Porsche hoped to adapt the principle for a small sports car of their own. Another Porsche in-house project at this time, though it did not reach prototype stage, was a shortened four-cylinder version of the 911 engine, perhaps to power this new sports car.

Volkswagen itself was in financial decline, however, and in September 1971 Rudolf Leiding replaced Kurt Lotz as chief executive. Within weeks he cancelled the EA 266 development, ordering the prototypes to be destroyed. As a sop he instigated the development of the EA 425, the intended successor to the Volkswagen-Porsche 914 model; being a joint stock off-shoot of both companies, based in Ludwigsburg but built by Karmann, it would cost VW very little and was of relatively minor importance.

Significant decisions were also made in Zuffenhausen in 1971, though for entirely

Above left The Porsche factory in the Zuffenhausen suburb of Stuttgart. Taken in 1986, the aerial view shows Works I, the headquarters (rectangular block of buildings on the left side of the main road), Works II, the main assembly plant on the right of the highway, and Works III on the right. The old barrack buildings in the centre will be removed when Works V is completed on the site of the car park (left).

Left Artist's impression of the new Works V (left), where Porsche bodies will be made from 1988, with an overbridge crossing the main road to the paint shop in Works II.

different reasons. Dr Ferdinand 'Ferry' Porsche had decided to develop his company, and as a first step he invited members of the Porsche and cousin Piëch families to look elsewhere for employment. Dr Ernst Fuhrmann, the designer of the four-camshaft Carrera engine, was appointed 'spokesman for the board' in the summer of 1971 (today, his successor is the chief executive) and within 12 months the family members departed. Ing Piëch handed over the Weissach post to Dipl Ing Helmuth Bott, and Ferdinand 'Butzi' Porsche set off to form the independent Porsche Design company in Austria (his styling successor, Anatole 'Tony' Lapine, would report to Bott). The second son, Gerhard (Gerd) was a farmer with no active interest in the family firm but the third son, Hans-Peter, resigned from heading the production department, later to join 'Butzi' at Porsche Design.

Wolfgang was too young to have joined the firm then, studying economics in Stuttgart although today, a Doctor in Economics, he is perhaps being groomed to become the titular head of the company sometime in the future. Ferdinand Piëch, rather ironically, left Weissach to take up a post at Audi's Ingolstadt headquarters, and is now vice-chairman of Audi in charge of research and development. His uncle's summary of Piëch's nine years with Porsche was, 'His ambition and enthusiasm—though perhaps not always tempered by restraint—quickly became apparent.' His younger brother, Dr Michael Piëch, was with the company just a year, heading general management at Zuffenhausen.

The family members made immense contributions to Porsche. 'Butzi' gave the 911 its ageless appeal, and Ferdinand Piëch developed the six-cylinder engine into a classic design; he also developed the mighty 917 racing cars, at a cost that far exceeded his uncle's expectations! There were many disagreements how-

Left *Professor Dr Ernst Fuhrmann, chief executive of Porsche from 1972 to 1980. In his time the four and eight-cylinder ranges were developed and produced . . . but the 911's days were numbered.*

Right *Professor Fuhrmann's legacy to Porsche was a greatly expanded range of sports cars. The model range in 1980 included the 911 SC and, clockwise, the Turbo model introduced in 1975, the 911 Targa, the 928 model introduced in 1977, the 928S introduced in 1979, the 924 introduced in 1975 and the 924 Turbo introduced in 1978.*

ever—'They are like sand in a well-oiled machine,' said Dr Porsche—and good men were being held down.

In August 1972 the final phase of the reorganization was completed. The limited partnership KG (Kommanditgesellschaft) status was turned into joint-stock AG (Aktiengesellschaft) status. There were ten shareholders, principally Dr Ferdinand Porsche, his sister Louise Piëch, each with four children having equal holdings. There was a supervisory board headed by Dr Porsche with three family members and elected union representatives (the Aufsichtsrat), and reporting regularly to that was the Vorstand, or board of management. Its chairman was Dr Fuhrmann, recalled from the Goetze piston company, his deputy being finance director Heinz Branitzki.

One of the first decisions taken by Dr Fuhrmann, in October 1971, was to establish the general layout of the 928 model. It eventually appeared nearly six years later, delayed by the oil crisis and downturn in business. It was designed to have a water-cooled engine at the front, trans-axle drive at the rear, with the two connected by a rigid torque tube. The engine would be of 5-litre capacity with a target of 300 bhp, and rather larger than the 911. It might be the 911's successor, but no-one was really thinking that far ahead, not enough to be sure. On the 20-year life span which was normal at Porsche, the 911's days might end in 1984, possibly forced out by future legislations concerning pollution, noise control, crash safety and who knew what else.

The development contract for the EA 425 came as a very useful bonus, allowing Porsche to develop the trans-axle system on a smaller scale and, particularly, to establish that possible problems with vibration in the long torque shaft could

easily be overcome. Starting a few weeks after project 928, the EA 425 was given priority, and soon some very unusual BMWs and Opels were on the streets testing new transmission and suspension systems.

In Porsche's book the EA 425 was a Volkswagen, and prototypes wore VW's badge on the nose. The Volkswagen-Porsche project and its type 914 model had never been a favourite of Dr Porsche, and the 115,600 built were never included in Porsche's totals. Nearly all were powered by Volkswagen's four-cylinder engines, anyway, just 2,750 being built with Porsche's 2-litre flat-six in 1970, and only 357 in 1971. At DM20,000 the 914/6 was a little less expensive than the faster 2.2-litre Porsche 911, and Porsche devotees made their preference clear.

In 1970/71 the American dollar was in one of its periodic declines, affecting German companies and the strong Deutschmark quite badly. VW-Audi, with its high US-based turnover, reckoned that every pfennig dropped on the dollar exchange cost it DM25 million a year. In the wake of the first oil crisis in 1974, and again in 1979/82 during the deeper recession, Porsche's dependence on the American market would cause severe problems although, as Peter Schutz explains later in this chapter, ways have now been found to cope with such fluctuations. Certainly, throughout the 1970s all the German manufacturers, including Porsche, were excessively cost and price conscious when specifying for the American market, and that led to its own problems.

It was the 1974 slump which brought Volkswagen close to bankruptcy that proved a turning-point for Porsche. Throughout his tenure of office, Rudolf Leiding had been as unsupportive of the VW-Porsche company in Ludwigsburg as Porsche itself, and when he was forced to lay off engineers in Wolfsburg his mind turned again to the matter of Porsche's contract to develop Volkswagens. Early in 1972 he had summarily cancelled the Piëch-designed EA 266 saloon when it was close to launch as the Beetle's successor, and chose instead to accelerate development of the Golf. In 1973 he cancelled the engineering/development contract as well, a decision that, although half expected by Porsche's board, still came as a shock.

The EA 425 sports car contract was continued, but that was really all that remained of the relationship. This left VW-Porsche Vertriebsgesellschaft GmbH, headed by Otto-Erich Filius and K Schneider, in a difficult position, since VW and Porsche each held a 50 per cent stake in a company that had been responsible both for development and marketing.

VW-Porsche continued to market the 914 model and prepare for the launch of the Volkswagen EA 425 sports car, though VW's own Scirocco coupé launched in March 1974 served as a warning that the EA 425 was not a priority project. In the autumn of 1974 Dr Fuhrmann sent VW-Porsche's sales manager, Lars-Roger Schmidt, to Leiding to propose that Porsche should take over the EA 425 project and launch it as a Porsche, 'but I got thrown out,' says Schmidt.

Leiding's days were numbered anyway, as VW neared bankruptcy, and in December the chief stepped down on the grounds of ill-health. He was replaced by Toni Schmücker, and in January 1975 Schmidt returned to Wolfsburg with the proposal about the EA 425. This time it was accepted, a fact which counters the popular belief that Schmücker himself cancelled EA 425. 'It wasn't his baby,' says Schmidt. 'He had enough problems on his plate, and he liked our proposal.' This entailed EA 425 returning to Porsche in its entirety, and Porsche paying a royalty on the first 100,000 cars built rather than a lump sum; even so, Porsche still had to stake out DM100 million for the takeover, which included buying-out VW's half-share of the Ludwigsburg operation and the launch of the 924.

For VW it was an attractive deal. Without it Schmücker would certainly have closed the former NSU plant at Neckarsulm, the least profitable of all VW's factories where the Audi 100 and remnants of the NSU Ro80 were made. Better still, VW's Salzgitter plant would produce some 20,000 engines a year for the Porsche 924. These would be specially-developed versions of the type 831 water-cooled four-cylinder, as used in the LT 28 light van, and sold in short block form to American Motors for the Gremlin. At full 2-litre capacity and with Bosch K-Jetronic fuel injection, the type 831 developed 125 bhp throughout its Porsche life-span from 1975 to 1985, though Porsche themselves would produce special versions with turbo-charging.

Additionally the 924 would incorporate Audi's four-speed manual or three-speed automatic transmissions and steering, suspension and brakes from the VW-Audi parts bins. Even such things as instruments and door handles came from VW, strongly recalling the origins of the much-loved Porsche 356 sports car.

Schmidt was 'called to the Board' of Porsche as sales director in 1974, with the winding-up of VW-Porsche, and only then did he learn very much about Projekt 928. 'At VW-Porsche we were the enemy, and we were told as little as possible about it,' he recalls. 'The family was fighting about it, there was no money available for development, it was clearly going above the budget, and would cost much more than the 911 it was supposed to replace.' Schmidt found himself with the power of veto over the eight-cylinder model, but Dr Fuhrmann had the Vorstand firmly in line so not surprisingly he went with the majority, albeit with deep reservations.

At Weissach, Porsche's showcase research and development centre 16 miles (25 km) to the west of Stuttgart, the new Hexagon main building was opened in 1974, where the staff level had risen to 900. They were involved in government contracts, developing the Leopard tank and the Weasel half-track scout car, and of course with Porsche's own developments and with racing, but the loss of the VW development contract was a serious blow.

Porsche's problem was reliance on the 911 model, then ten years old and made at a rate of 15-16,000 a year in good times. In 1974 demand slumped dangerously, some 11,800 being built in that model year, and Porsche only broke even financially. Things worsened in the 1975 model year with production falling below 9,000 cars, of which the Americans bought a meagre 4,732. The 911 Turbo model had been developed and launched, and was to prove successful beyond Porsche's dreams, but that alone could not cure the blight.

The 911 Turbo was one of the outstanding successes of Dr Fuhrmann's nine-year reign, for it was he who insisted that the 400 examples needed to gain Group 4 acceptance for racing in 1976 must be highly equipped and luxurious flagships. The wisdom of this is borne out by the fact that the type 930 Turbo became a cult-status supercar, with sales averaging between 1,000 and 2,000 a year to this day.

The decision to take the EA 425/Porsche 924 project on board was inevitable in the circumstances, since to have started a new design would have taken some years and incurred high expense. The takeover delayed the launch very little as the special production line at Neckarsulm was assigned to Porsche; the bodies were made there, and other than seating very few components actually emanated from Zuffenhausen. Porsche had designed the 924 and developed the trans-axle system, and it had been styled in Tony Lapine's department at Weissach. So, could Porsche's customers ask for more?

Yes and no is the ambivalent reply. Porsche enthusiasts were deeply suspicious of the 924, drawing attention to its 'van engine' which was not conspicuously smooth at high speeds, its four widely-spaced gear ratios, its slightly frail braking system with drums at the rear, and less than perfectly-refined noise levels. Perhaps the styling was a little effeminate too, and proud owners who joined Porsche Clubs around the world were disappointed to realize that they were the objects of curiosity, even pity.

However, the 911 was making a strong revival, and continued to cater for the aficionados. In the 1976 model year Porsche's production exceeded 20,000 for the first time in the company's history, numbering 8,344 early production 924s, most of which were sold in the German market, precisely 10,001 six-cylinders (7,313 of the 911, 1,531 higher performance Carreras and 1,157 Turbos), plus 2,000 examples of the revived four-cylinder 912 model, reintroduced to the American market for one year to fill the gap between the demise of the 914/4 and the new 924. Porsche's overall profit trebled that year, though only to DM7.4 million.

The real benefit of the 924 was in bringing 100,000 new customers to Porsche over a five-year period: people who could never have afforded one before but had, perhaps, a long-standing ambition to 'join the family'. Others might never have thought of buying a Porsche at all but were attracted by the realistic price of DM24,000 (initially £7,000 in Britain) and by the clean styling. With back seats that would fold flat to increase the luggage area it was a truly versatile car, over-geared for economy and with outstanding road-holding. In all these areas Porsche's objectives were achieved, the trans-axle system proved the benefits of having equal front/rear weight distribution, and with each year that passed the 924 became a little quieter and more refined, and eventually very desirable.

The second half of the 1970s was a peaceful and prosperous time for Porsche, with a good deal of activity. In the 1977 model year production rose to 37,435 worldwide, with the American market making a strong recovery and taking 20,757 cars. The 924 model became the most successful in the company's history with 23,180 sales in the one year, company profits shooting up from DM7.5 million to a healthy DM17.0 million.

The 928 model was announced at the Geneva Show in March 1977 and created such a favourable impression that it was named 'Car of the Year' by an international jury of motoring writers. This is Europe's ultimate accolade, and immediately created a black market with early production models changing hands at over list price. In 1978, the 924 Turbo model was announced with 170 bhp, much more the sort of car for which enthusiasts would hanker.

Worldwide, the dealer network was out of the 1974/75 trough and was expanding strongly. In Britain, where Porsche owned 60 per cent of the importer's shareholding and the Aldington family the remaining 40 per cent, sales exceeded 1,000 cars for the first time, more than half of them 924s. (John Aldington, managing director of PCGB subsequently sold his shareholding to the factory in April 1987, and resigned his executive responsibility.) The value of a prosperous dealer network can never be under-estimated, and Porsche's takeover of the EA 425 project was one of the soundest decisions made in the company's history. A year later Mitsuwa Motors in Tokyo also sold 1,000 Porsches for the first time, though with 40 dealerships rather than 26 in Britain, and Porsche Cars Great Britain Limited firmly established itself as the third largest in the world. Typically, 50 per cent of all Porsche production would be sold in America, 25-30 per cent in Germany, and the remainder in the rest of the world with Britain, France, Italy, Japan, Austria and Switzerland making the strongest impact.

In Zuffenhausen, though, all was not as well as it seemed. The old World War II barrack buildings badly needed replacing and the 911s continued to be built in the same old way. The din of dozens of panel beaters at work (most of them Turkish or Greek 'guestworkers') was appalling, and only the new 928 extension at Works II provided any haven. There some 20 eight-cylinder cars could be

Porsche's 911 assembly track in 1987 was little improved since the 356 models went along it in 1950. The new Works V to be opened in 1988 should transform the working conditions.

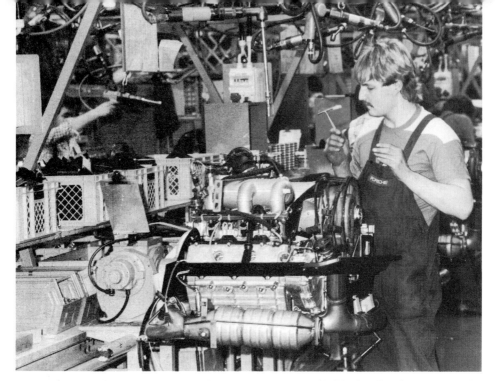

Despite the volume of production Porsche's engines are assembled by hand, technicians usually working in pairs. All four, six and eight-cylinder power units are built in Zuffenhausen, and bench-tested before installation.

made each working day, up to 5,000 per year were being constructed, and Dr Fuhrmann was more sure than ever that the much-developed 928 would indeed be the 911's successor by the mid-1980s. New four-cylinder models would fill the gap at the lower end, the 944 Turbo for instance with similar performance to the 911's, and Porsche's products would be thoroughly modernized.

That was not Dr Porsche's viewpoint, though. To him and to a quarter of a million people who had ever bought a new 911, the six-cylinder model was the epitome of sports car pleasure. When he said that the 911 would continue as long as there was a demand he really meant it; but at that time Dr Fuhrmann anticipated that the four- and eight-cylinder models would push the 911 below the waves, to a level that would be uneconomic to keep in production.

Furthermore, argued Fuhrmann, new legislations around the world would not be framed in contexts that favoured a rear-engined, air-cooled sports car. Emission controls would soon lock the 911 Carrera Turbo model (930) out of America from 1 January 1980. In fact, noise control was becoming a topical subject, it was impossible to defrost the windows as quickly as a new European regulation demanded. . . it rather seemed that Fuhrmann gave up, deciding that future regulations would be beyond economic development of the 911.

The relationship between Dr Porsche and Dr Fuhrmann cooled, and was virtually severed when Dr Porsche moved his office to the marketing department in Ludwigsburg in 1978. They were not seen together in public, even avoided each other, and it was Dr Fuhrmann on his own who went to Monte Carlo in January 1978 to collect the Car of the Year award for the 928 from Prince

Rainier. It was an auspicious occasion that Dr Porsche would have enjoyed, for just prior to the ceremony Jean-Pierre Nicolas most unexpectedly won the Monte Carlo Rally in the Almeras brothers' 911, having made the wisest decisions about tyres for various difficult stages. This was the 911's fourth Monte Carlo Rally success but the first without any support from the factory, and Dr Fuhrmann was encouraged to send a 911 team to tackle the East African Safari Rally once more. This was not quite so successful, netting second and fourth places in the overall classification.

Also in sport the Renault team vanquished the Porsche factory's 936 team at Le Mans, at its third attempt, and at that point investment in motor racing was cut to the bone. The 935/78 had been developed expensively, to race only three times, and the water-cooled four-valve cylinder-head technology was also transferred to the 936 model. The race programme was virtually halted after Porche's Le Mans defeat in 1978—an honourable one, it should be said—and customers carried the flag with the 935 model, notably developed by Kremer Racing and by Reinhold Joest. Porsche tackled Le Mans again in 1979 with the 936s backed by Essex Petroleum, but had run only one warm-up race, at Silverstone, which showed that tyre trouble could prevent success, as could the rather weak five-speed transmissions. Both works Porsches retired from the 1979 event, and the wet race produced another surprise winner, the Kremer Porsche 935, the first time in many years that a production-based car had won the classic event.

In 1980 Porsche fielded a team of 924 Carrera GTRs, racing developments of the 924 Turbo and Carrera GT, leaving the 936s at base. This caused anguish in Porsche's boardroom and throughout the company, the more so since the 924 model itself, powered by the Volkswagen originated engine, had a very limited life expectancy, and furthermore was not properly developed. One finished in sixth place, others had valve troubles as anticipated, and the race would almost certainly have been won by a works 936, had it been entered.

The climate in which the key relationship in the company soured is easy to understand. In the summer of 1979, so the official story goes, Dr Fuhrmann had intimated to Dr Porsche that he would step down from his post when a suitable successor could be found. Fuhrmann was an engineer, an ideal man to run an engineer-led company but ill-equipped to deal with the vicissitudes of the market-place. It is unlikely that the award of a Professor's seat at the University of Vienna to Dr Fuhrmann in 1979 was greeted with anything approaching enthusiasm in Dr Porsche's office.

More storm clouds were gathering. Production to July 1979 reached an absolute record of 41,350 cars, but for the second year in succession demand in America for the 924 model had fallen, though compensated partly by good demand for the 928. The Americans, more forthrightly than the Europeans, thought the 924 to be a 'lemon', and US sales of the four-cylinder model fell from a peak of 13,700 in 1977 to 8,400 in 1979, and to 5,400 in 1980; sales of the 928 in 1978-1980 averaged 1,500 annually, however.

The 924 had done its job, reaching 100,000 sales in five years, and would achieve only 38,000 sales in the next five years once out of the American market. The 944 model, which would be a remarkable success, was still two years away and Porsche would suffer along with everyone else in the depression. In particular it was the American market that would cause most grief, the DM/Dollar ratio having fallen to an all-time low of 1.72, and Porsche was hit harder than Mercedes-Benz and BMW.

Then more than ever cost-cutting was the order of the day. In 1980 production fell by an agonizing 25 per cent to 31,138, of which the Americans took fewer than 12,000, or 38 per cent. The US dealers, numbering around 350, were awash with the full Porsche range (at one time the surplus exceeded 4,000 cars) and each, on average, sold 34 cars. In Britain by contrast sales were continuing to rise, the 26 dealers selling a total of 2,000 cars, an average of 77 each, and good profits were continuing to be made.

One of the problems in the States was felt to be the sales pitch. Imports were controlled by Audi-Volkswagen and Porsches were sold alongside Audi saloons, Volkswagen Rabbits and Sciroccos. Less well-informed customers would perceive Porsches to be rather upmarket and very expensive versions of these ranges, comparing the 924 unfavourably with the Scirocco and the Mazda RX-7, for instance, on instant price valuations. From Stuttgart sales director Lars-Roger Schmidt went with a 'task force' sales team to gee-up the dealers and their staffs to extol Porsche values, Porsche workmanship, and generally to motivate the entire structure. Their groundwork was excellent for climbing out of the recession, but from midway through 1979 to early 1982 there was little but heartbreak.

As ever, cost and pricing seemed to be the keys. When asked by the author in 1980 why Porsche did not fit gas struts to the 924's engine lid, Mr. Bott exclaimed that this would cost 24 Deutschmarks. For the same reason the 924 did not have an interior release for the glass tailgate, another item on which the Mazda scored. To all intents and purposes Porsche was trying to compete, on price, with the Mazda RX-7 and VW Scirocco, and with Mercedes and BMW coupés further up the range. It was a David and Goliath task, and on this occasion David was losing heavily to the volume manufacturers. In 1980 a 'cheaper' version of the 928 was introduced, with vinyl instead of leather on the dashboard and with air-conditioning as an option. It attracted no positive interest whatsoever, merely adverse comment.

Pricing has always been a source of contention within Porsche, inevitably since comparatively low volume necessarily raises unit costs, and all the while the engineers push away at technological frontiers. When the Mark is steady or weak against foreign currencies, especially the dollar, the problem is pushed aside but periodically—in 1974, in 1980 and in 1987—it returns to haunt the management.

Sales director Schmidt fought a furious battle over the 928's pricing with Dr Fuhrmann and Herr Bott, pointing out that it was supposed to cost 10 per cent more than the 911, but had to be priced 30 per cent above the six-cylinder. This argument was to be re-run with Peter Schutz in 1981 when the 944 was nearing its launch. Schutz wanted to introduce the 944 at an attractive 'introductory' price and had a figure of DM35,000 in mind, although finance director Heinz Branitzki's figures put the true sales price at DM42,000.

The 944 was, in fact, introduced at DM39,000, a figure that pleased the dealer network and its customers but left a bad feeling in the boardroom. Matters came to a head two years later when Schmidt fought another battle, this time over the 944 Turbo's pricing. 'It was supposed to be 10 per cent cheaper than the 911 Carrera—that was the board's decision,' he states. 'When all the figures were worked out it was 10 per cent more expensive than the 911, so a very bad mistake had been made. I thought the model should be shelved completely, but I was over-ruled on that one. In the States it was priced halfway between the 944 and the 911, and while the dollar was strong they could stand that. . . but now (in 1987) it's a big problem.'

When the dollar dropped to DM1.69 one day midway through 1980, Schmidt and Branitzki felt there was little they could do but pray. . . and sink half a bottle of Scotch! The terrible slump in sales that followed was a real crisis-point for Porsche, and coupled with the fierce battles he regularly engaged on pricing it took its toll on Schmidt. He resigned his position in 1983, after losing another war.

This last battle concerned the restructuring of the American dealer network, which Schutz intended to take the form of a Porsche-owned organization. Schmidt's less expensive plan was to form a joint-stock company with VW's Audi division, effectively separating Audi sales from VW's in the States. Carl Hahn, VW's chairman, gave his broad approval but the proposal was dashed by Schutz, and Schmidt departed soon afterwards. He is now, in 1987, at the head of Jaguar Deutschland, a make competing with Porsche for wealthy customers in the German market. He is remembered by former colleagues as 'the guy who was always arguing' though none doubted that he battled with absolute conviction.

At this dark time the Weissach research and development centre was giving encouraging results. By 1980 nearly 100 outside contracts were being handled by a staff of 1,000 and turnover, at DM172 million, accounted for 13.9 per cent of the company's annual budget; around 40 per cent of the work was for clients, and was reliably profitable. One contract which came close to signature, and aroused a lot of comment, was the development of a new family car as a joint venture with the Austrian government. Austrian Chancellor Bruno Kreisky, correctly judging the emergence of Spain as a car-producing nation, felt that Austria should have its own industry too. Professor Porsche had worked for the old Austro-Daimler concern, and good progress was made towards founding a joint-stock company to produce the Austro-Porsche.

In the end Porsche decided not to proceed, mainly because its name should not be associated too strongly with a family car. Memories of the VW-Porsche were still strong, and although the Porsche family is Austrian, ties of heritage were not strong enough to quell the doubts. Over-capacity throughout the European industry in the 1980s tends to confirm that the decision was absolutely correct, although at a later date Porsche was happy enough for its name to appear on the engines developed at Weissach for the Spanish SEAT company.

_____ A new start _____

While members of the Porsche family other than Dr Porsche were not actively involved in the running of the company, Dr Porsche was receiving advice from his youngest son Dr Wolfgang Porsche. His advice was that a change of top management was needed, and the sooner the better. Dr Wolfgang was not, like his elders, an engineer but a doctor of commerce, his degree obtained almost inevitably at the University of Vienna. Unusually, perhaps, he held a key position at Daimler-Benz as head of the finance department concerned with North America. There was no conflict of interest, but his knowledge of a well-run and successful manufacturer's operations in the States was of critical importance.

In the summer of 1980 Dr Porsche's search for a successor to Prof Dr Fuhrmann reached a successful conclusion. Discussions with Peter W Schutz, then a board member of the Klöckner-Humboldt-Deutz (KHD) industrial plant and machinery company, reached a meeting of minds. Schutz's philosophy would be to expand the company, to perpetuate the 911 and to invest heavily in production and research facilities; in fact to take the Porsche company on to an entirely new plane. Talks continued through the autumn and in December 1980 there was a brief, bald statement that from 1 January 1981, Mr Schutz would be the new chief executive. Professor Fuhrmann, thanked for his contribution, would retire at the age of 61 to lecture at the University of Vienna.

A less likely successor was hard to imagine. Schutz's family had fled the Nazi regime in 1938, when Peter was eight years of age, and later settled in Chicago. The head of the family, a doctor, had to take menial jobs while learning the language. Peter Schutz gained an engineering degree at the Illinois Institute of Technology in Detroit, joined the Caterpillar company as a research and development engineer, and later joined the Cummins Diesel company, rising to head the truck engine division.

The engineering background was important in getting Schutz to the interview stage, but is entirely subsidiary to his outgoing personality, his ability (indeed his creed) for motivation and his tendency to think forward and laterally at the same time. Although Porsche's Vorstand was mainly young and had not led a sheltered life, the impact of a rather brash American with little knowledge of Porsche's background and methods was considerable. To Schutz everything was 'do-able'. 'Why not?' was his frequent exasperated response to stone-wallers. Everything regarded as sacred, inviolate and 'company policy' was opened up, examined and often rejected.

Soon there were sweeping changes in the boardroom as Schutz brought in his own men, but these were not hatchet jobs. Finance director Heinz Branitzki stayed at his post, he and research director Helmuth Bott quickly earning Schutz's total support. However in 1981 Dr Heiko Lange was recruited from ITT to head the personnel department according to Schutz's modern philosophy, and in January

1983 Professor Dr Rudi Noppen was recruited from KHD at the age of 39 to direct the production and supply departments. The departure of Lars-Roger Schmidt from sales proved a problem in 1983, and it was nearly a year before a successor was named in Mario-Jon Nadelcu. . . but he only lasted a year anyway.

These were turbulent times, full of expansion, excitement and opportunity. At times the management did not know what to expect next from their shoot-from-the-hip executive, but the 'Messiah with the golden tongue' soon proved to have the Midas touch.

In an interview, Peter Schutz recalled his introduction to the company. 'If I had not believed in the policy of growth I would not have joined the company. I had conversations with friends and people I respect in the fall of 1980, and it was pretty clear to me the way it would go before I even started here. Different managers and different leaders have different talents, and are good at different things.

'The business was in need of a fundamental reorientation. If I were to over-simplify the state of mind of the company when I first came to it, it was that the company viewed itself as serving a gradually shrinking market for high technology sports cars. The strategy was to capture an increasing share of an ever decreasing market, described in business books as "cash cow". Those text books tell you that you minimize your investments and maximize your margins, until the market finally disappears.

'Tending a "cash cow" takes certain skills, but it is not something that I would like to do, or would do well. I feel at home in a growing entrepreneurial environment, and because that's where I like to be, that's where I do well. Professor Porsche sensed the same things. . . obviously we talked a lot in the summer and fall of 1980, and that's the basis on which we got together. The nucleus of that concept was really the prerequisite for my employment.

'I gave this a lot of consideration and decided that Porsche was not in a shrinking market. The Porsche customer is an entrepreneur, whose segment in the Western world is growing dramatically. The successful businessman is no longer the chief executive of a steel company, rather the owner of a McDonald's franchise. We have smaller business units but with a large number of successful entrepreneurs. This cuts through all the old notions and includes the fast food industry, the athletes, the entertainers, to geniuses who started the high-tech businesses. The whole growth is in the entrepreneurial market, and even in the large companies the most successful people are the ones who view themselves in an entrepreneurial sense. In IBM for instance there might be someone who got a hold of the personal computer department and regards his role in the company almost as an entre-preneur, away from the mainstream of the traditional business, exploring new economic opportunities.

'In London the "Big bang" as you called it has created a whole new market for Porsches. So you see, it was my perception that we were not serving a shrinking market at all, so we had to reorient our strategy completely. For instance we became more active in racing, with the throw-off in both image and technology for the company. We revitalized the motivation of a lot of people in the company, and went from a sort of holding-on philosophy to an aggressive, growth-oriented philosophy. Fundamentally that's the change that we underwent when I joined Porsche.'

Results speak louder than words and within weeks of Schutz's appointment the engine was pulling the train again. In January 1981 Porsche was at its very lowest ebb with production, in the 1981 model year to July, down to 28,015. Fewer than 8,000 Porsches were sold in America although the de-stocking campaign was beginning to be successful. The number of employees bottomed out at 4,900 and profits (not a reliable figure) levelled off at DM10 million.

Several factors would help the recovery, most notably the rise in value of the US dollar enjoyed by all the leading European exporting manufacturers. In Britain, Jaguar made an even more remarkable recovery almost from the edge of the grave, and companies like Mercedes, BMW, Volvo and Saab entered a golden era. For Porsche the new prosperity, led by the outstanding success of the 944 model, created revenue that would allow a 'spend-spend' investment programme which will be completed with the opening of the new Works V body plant in Zuffenhausen early in 1988.

In June 1982 a new, fully computer-operated parts distribution warehouse was opened at Works II at a cost of DM50 million (that, of course, had been commissioned and accounted in Prof Furhmann's time). DM23 million was invested in a new 'environment centre' at Weissach, the most advanced emissions laboratory in Europe where 50 per cent of its capacity would be allocated to customer contracts. In 1986 the vitally-needed new paint shop was opened at Works II (DM100 million), and a few weeks later a new full-size wind tunnel was baptized at Weissach, completing a further DM37 million expenditure.

These developments will be described in greater detail, but the central figure for investments in the 1980s is in excess of DM1,000 million, an astonishing sum for such a relatively small company. The main programme was planned to end early in 1988 with the opening of a huge new body plant, built across the highway from Works II and connected to it by a tracked road bridge leading straight to the new paint shop. The investment here is DM125 million, and its opening will complete the revolution that was required to modernize the Porsche company.

Peter Schutz explained, 'Expansion began when I took office, but until 1986 it was simply a question of using the capacity that was already in place. In the first four years it was a question of utilizing existing capacity, and it was not until 1985 that we took the whole operation up a gear to two shifts, and opened the new paint facility that broke a bottleneck in the production system. And now the new bodyshop which is taking shape across the street will be our last step in modernizing the Zuffenhausen facilities.

'We now have enough capacity to meet the demand for our products for quite some time. Although it isn't generally done in Germany we have the option, if the need arises, to go to a three-shift operation. I think we now have the capacity to meet the demand that we're able to generate.

'However the main thrust of the modernization at Zuffenhausen, including the two-shift operation, was more a question of updating the workplaces and modernizing the plant to be commensurate with what you should reasonably expect in the 1980s. If you look at some of the old plant, the barracks, those are working conditions and working equipment that are not up-to-date, and not commensurate with what a modern factory worker can expect to have in the way of tools. We have installed a lot of expensive machinery, including some robots to do the dirty jobs, so we have used the period of the high dollar to undertake a lot of investment that had been neglected. The new chassis plant at Works V is the last of the "biggies". We're well equipped now, facility-wise, for the future.'

Going back to 1981, Peter Schutz began to make his presence felt within days. His first major decision, he says, was to repeal the death sentence on the 911 model and to authorize Weissach to produce a 'Studie' which appeared at the Frankfurt Show nine months later. This had a rather rudimentary four-wheel drive system involving a driveshaft running forward from the gearbox (easy, because the engine was overhung at the back) to a 924 Turbo differential between the front wheels. Dr Porsche has subsequently revealed that four-wheel drive was an active development in the 1970s, and even neared production readiness before being shelved. Of more immediate interest was the convertible body, a forerunner of the 911 Cabriolet model which was shown in definitive form at the Geneva Show in March 1982, prior to full production.

On the competitions front, a new department was formed to prepare the 936 model for Le Mans, the only major change being the adoption of the old Can-Am four-speed gearbox which, though not having suitable ratios, was rated to 1,000 bhp and would be totally reliable. The 936 driven by Jacky Ickx and Derek Bell won the 24-Hour race with ease, and soon after that Schutz gave the go-ahead for the development of the 956 model designed specifically for the new Group C formula to be introduced in 1982. That, as we now know, was the most successful race programme in Porsche's entire history, the 956 and its successor, the 962, proving virtually unbeatable in the seasons 1982 to 1986.

A new competitions centre at Weissach, away from the main buildings and close to the test track, was headed by Peter Falk, a senior member of the research department, and soon became known as 'Falkland'. Here was much-needed elbow room for the 10 engineers and 30 mechanics who formed the permanent staff engaged in the design, development, testing and race preparation of the factory's Group C cars, and the Formula 1 engines under contract to TAG and McLaren International.

The announcement of the 944 model in 1981 was another major factor in the turnaround, and within two years it reached and maintained a production level in excess of 50 per cent of Porsche's annual output. In the 1983 model year, the first full year of export to America, over 14,000 Porsche 944s crossed the Atlantic, and in the 1985 model year 944 production reached an all-time record of 27,460 units, comfortably exceeding the 924 in its prime year. To Porsche's workforce should be added 2,000 Audi-employed staff producing the 944 and 924S, inferring that the four-cylinder range is not as profitable as it would be if produced entirely by Porsche, although all four, six and eight-cylinder power units are manufactured in Zuffenhausen.

In 1982 there was strong recovery in all markets, stimulated by the 944. Two hundred new jobs were created at Weissach, many in the new environment centre, and Porsche's payroll rose to 5,350. Turnover rose by 27 per cent to a record DM1,488 million and profits rose by a factor of 3.7 to DM37.6 million. The workforce was pleasantly surprised to be awarded a shared 'performance bonus' amounting to DM5 million, something that had never happened before, and formed the opinion that this American was not such a bad guy after all!

The 1982-83 financial and model years confirmed the strong recovery, production rising by an unprecedented 38 per cent to 45,240 cars. Exports to America exceeded 20,000 cars for the first time since 1977 and profits rose by 85 per cent to DM69.6 million, although investments had risen to slightly over DM131 million. In the first year of Schutz's appointment, investments had risen by 50 per cent from DM80 million to DM125.7 million, but this new peak was to prove merely a plateau as a sum in excess of DM250 million was set aside for the 1984 financial year.

Capital spending on buildings, equipment and the development of new models was responsible for the major part, the 911 Cabriolet having been well received, and the 959 was well on the way to presentation at the Frankfurt Show in September 1983, the most technologically-advanced road car of its time. At this stage the 'supercar' was referred to as the 'Gruppe B', an ultimate production-based competitions car that could win rallies or races with equal aplomb. The power unit was developed from that of the 956 racing car, with 2.85-litre capacity and developing from 450 bhp in road trim to more than 650 bhp for competitions. To apply all that power, from an overhung rear engine, the Gruppe B 959 would have an amazingly complex four-wheel drive system employing an electronically-controlled, infinitely variable centre differential. The suspension characteristics would be controlled electronically too, and the power would be transmitted by a new six-speed gearbox. In order to have the car homologated though, at least 200 would have to be built and sold . . . that would cause some agonizing problems in the years to come.

Production levels were raised all round, squeezing every last car out of the antiquated lines. At Zuffenhausen the total capacity was raised to 71 cars per day, the 911 lines producing 53 cars instead of 45, and the 928S line 21 instead of 18. The 4.5-litre 928 had been discontinued as demand for the more powerful, and much more expensive 4.7-litre 928S was still greater than supply. At Neckarsulm a double-shift was introduced to raise four-cylinder production from 72 to 130 cars per day, all but a handful the new 944 model as the 924 went into its final year.

For the record, in the 1983 model year exports to America rose by 76 per cent to 20,235, although this was no more than 45.4 per cent of total production. The German home market accounted for 12,200 Porsches (27 per cent), Britain for 3,334 cars (7.2 per cent), France 2,106 (4.3 per cent), Switzerland and Italy 1,400 cars and 3.1 per cent apiece.

Two significant things happened in 1983 causing fundamental shifts in the Porsche business. At the start of the year Schutz caused a furore in America by announcing that when the firm's contract with Audi-Volkswagen expired in August 1984, Porsche would set up its own distribution network, pruning out the weaker dealers and forming new ones in key areas. It was entirely logical and must have been foreseen, but the dealer body rose up in arms and threats of writs flew in all directions. Then in November Ernst Piëch, one of Dr Porsche's Austrian hotel-owning nephews, broke the news to the family that he wished to sell his 9.5 per cent shareholding, valued at DM100 million, to the Kuwaiti owned Al-Mal and Saudi owned ABS Daus banks. The entire family closed ranks and agreed to buy this holding, but within weeks Dr Porsche's sister, Louise Piëch, announced that she too would sell out to the same consortium. The remaining eight family members found that they could not buy the second parcel—and the ructions would have provided an excellent script for the Dallas or Dynasty soap operas!

On 17 April 1984, a block of non-voting shares in Dr Ing hc F Porsche AG was placed on the Stuttgart, Frankfurt and Munich stock exchanges raising the nominal capital value of the company from DM50 million to DM70 million, of which half was offered to the public. The shares were bought eagerly, each nominal DM50 share valued at DM1,100 initially, and overnight Porsche had 35,000 share-holders instead of merely ten! Power and control of the company remained firmly in the family's hands and a crisis was averted.

That year was significant in more ways. In September Dr Ferdinand Porsche was conferred a Professor's seat at the University of Stuttgart on his 75th birthday, the honour bestowed by Lothar Späth, Prime Minister of the State of Baden-Württemberg, and the architect of the Porsche manufacturing company finally had his due reward. The title of the company, however, would not be changed.

Earlier in the year Porsche had been affected by a metalworkers' strike, which lasted for five weeks in the Spring and lost the company an estimated 5,660 cars valued at DM270 million. The IGM union chose Stuttgart as the centre of its dispute in order to affect Mercedes, Porsche, Mahle, ZF, and the vital Robert Bosch company, bringing Germany's motor industry to a standstill, but there is no evidence that Porsche's workers had any enthusiasm for the strike at all. Overtime, including Saturdays, was worked once the situation returned to normal and the 1984 model year's production, including the popular 911 Carrera 3.2 model, was merely 1 per cent reduced at 44,773. Production at Zuffenhausen was further increased to 81 cars per day.

In September Porsche Cars North America was opened in Reno, Nevada, the Porsche company having a 96 per cent shareholding valued at DM65 million. A Canadian, John Cook, was appointed president of PCNA and a pragmatic approach had been taken to the appointment of new dealers, the number remaining constant at around 320. No contracts were cancelled arbitrarily, all writs were withdrawn, and the weaker dealers would simply not have their contracts renewed when they expired. American sales were now firmly established on the upper side of 20,000 and huge profits were being made as each strong dollar bought DM3.4.

With the quota of good luck that every successful man needs, Peter Schutz was firmly established in command of the Porsche company. His initial contract ran for three years to the end of 1983, and as evidence of their confidence in him the Supervisory Board negotiated a new five-year contract which would not expire until the end of 1988, by which time the major transformation of the company would be completed.

One of Schutz's leisure interests is aviation—he is a qualified instructor in light aircraft—and the use of Porsche six-cylinder engines in the Cardington based AD500 airship had resulted in a Certificate of Airworthiness being granted. Taking this a stage further, the 3.2-litre Carrera engine was further developed for light aircraft installation. Unusually one lever controlled both the throttle valve and the propellor pitch resulting in easier and safer operation with better economy. The certificate was granted in the summer of 1984, the PFM 3200 rated at 156 kW (212 bhp) at take-off and 147 kW (200 bhp) when cruising. Following a round-the-world trip in a Mooney aircraft the PFM went on sale in 1987 priced at $17,800, without the specially-designed propellor.

On the sporting front Porsche was earning fresh laurels every month. The year 1984 had begun with a fine victory in the Paris-Dakar Raid, René Metge's 911/959 easily outlasting a huge field of marathon desert runners. This was not a proper 959 since it had a normally-aspirated Carrera engine and a simplified, non-electronic four-wheel drive system, but many of the 959's new components passed the severe 11,000 kilometre test. Two years later Metge again won the Paris-Dakar in a definitive 959, proving beyond doubt such things as the turbo-charged, water-cooled engine, the electronically-split four-wheel drive system and the new six-speed gearbox.

On the race circuits in 1984 Niki Lauda and Alain Prost, in their TAG-powered Marlboro McLarens, were romping away in the Drivers' and Constructors' Championships, with a total of 12 wins in 16 races. For many years Porsche had dominated sports car endurance events, sometimes against negligible competition, but very few people outside Weissach really believed that Porsche could break straight into the fiercely-contested Formula 1 field and succeed against manufacturers such as Ferrari, Renault and Honda. Chief race engine designer Hans Mezger, working closely with Bosch engineers on the all-important engine management systems, had produced a winner within six months of the V6 engine's debut at Zandvoort, and confounded the critics.

In many ways, therefore, 1984 had been a year of achievement, creating ground-work for further progress. In 1985 a double-shift system was introduced at Zuffenhausen to raise production yet again, from 80 to 100 cars per day. Of these, 78 were 911s and 22 were 928s, while at Neckarsulm the production of four-cylinder cars, the 944 and the new 924S with its similar Porsche designed power unit, was speeded up from 132 to 140 cars per day. Reckoning that each year contains 240 working days, allowing for weekends, holidays and model changes, that gave a theoretical capacity of 23,000 911s and 928s at Zuffenhausen and 32,200 944s and 924Ss at Neckarsulm, a total of 55,200 Porsches in a full year, and this ideal target was almost met in the 1986 model year when for the second year in succession production topped the 50,000 mark at 53,625 cars.

Porsche's business was going well in other parts of the world, too. At Calcot,

Above *Porsche Cars Great Britain Ltd expanded again in 1985 when new premises were taken in Reading, Berkshire, to handle 4,000 sales per year. Within two years the Porsche factory acquired John Aldington's shareholding to make PCGB a 100 per cent subsidiary (and with it, AFN Limited which became the factory's only wholly-owned dealership).*

Below *By 1985 Porsche's model range had expanded again. Clockwise: the 928S was now the standard eight-cylinder model, the 944 had become the best-ever seller, and the 924 continued in production; the 911 Turbo continued to appeal, and the 911 range was augmented (in 1982) by the Cabriolet model. Alongside the Targa is the sport-equipped 911 Carrera.*

Reading, Porsche Cars Great Britain Limited open a large, futuristic import centre valued at £11 million to handle 3,500 sales per annum, the staff level moving towards the 200 mark. In America PCNA sold 28,671 cars in the 1986 financial year, although the exchange rate was beginning to fall from its peak and would seriously curtail profits, from an all-time high of DM120 million to just DM75.3 million. Early in 1987 John Cook would announce that he was talking to various European manufacturers, not then exporting to America, with a view to handling an additional franchise and make better use of the facilities available. Then Porsche controlled distribution in most of its major markets, America, Germany, Britain, France (Sonauto), Spain (Porsche España), and finally in Italy where sales had fallen in a disappointing way, and needed reviving. Stiff motor tax laws in Italy had much to do with the decline, the 924 and 924 Turbo having been popular models at under 2-litres, and the new 2.5-litre 924S was not exactly the model that the Italian dealers needed.

While production of the 944 reached a record level at 27,460 in 1985, two new versions were in the pipeline. The 944 Turbo, which could virtually match the performance of the 911 Carrera, was introduced in 1985 and the 16-valve 944S a year later, though the latter model, with higher performance than the 8-valve model noted particularly at the upper end of the power band, was not immediately as successful as Porsche had hoped.

There was no doubt, though, about the success of the 32-valve Porsche 928S-4, in many ways as advanced as the 959. With more power, now 320 bhp, and improved aerodynamics, the 928S-4 became the fastest model in Porsche's range, even outstripping the 911 Turbo; Al Holbert, Porsche's motor sports director in America, drove the newcomer virtually in standard form at 171 mph (274 km/h) on the Bonneville salt flats. Significantly his production car was equipped with full three-way catalytic equipment, underlining Porsche's stated policy of offering equal performance in all markets with new models.

Porsche was the first company to offer emission-free models with supercar performance, another great achievement by the Weissach engineers. In 1983 the Frankfurt Show had been overshadowed by talk of German and European legislations calling for catalytic equipment, and it had seemed then that the days of unrestricted high performance were numbered. Cars with emission equipment were fine for America, with its 55 mph (88 km/h) speed limit but would be slow, expensive and unreliable in European conditions, especially on the *Autobahnen* systems.

Thirty-six months of intensive development proved that the prognosis was incorrect. Experience with catalysers, notably the three-way system with Lambda probes, showed that they could be reliable, while massive improvements in computer technology (equal, probably, to the feat of reducing room-sized computers to pocket-calculator size) transformed the entire equation. Emission-controlled cars would be more expensive, certainly, but speed-loving customers had nothing to fear in the new legislations. Porsche, with the majority, would move on to address the next problem, that of noise control, in which the Swiss had taken a lead.

In September 1986 Dipl Ing Helmuth Bott was conferred a Professorship by the University of Stuttgart, in his 15th year as Porsche's research and development director, the period having seen profound changes and advances in the technological field. Now Porsche had 120 outside contracts (never having lost one, according to Prof Bott) valued at DM100 million annually; most clients cannot be named for business reasons, unless they themselves disclose a contract, but they included the German government, Lada, Seat, Ford, Volvo and an interesting contract to design ergonomically the cockpit layout of the A 310 European Airbus.

The level of staffing at Weissach increased rapidly in the 1980s from a base-point of 1,000 in 1981 to 2,300 in 1986, nearly 30 per cent of Porsche's payroll. About 40 per cent of the work carried out there is on behalf of clients ('it should be more', said Bott, 'but our own requirements increase all the time'), and the revenue is normally between 11 per cent and 14 per cent of the company's total. As well as the environment centre, Weissach has recently been equipped with its wind tunnel, a new crash-test laboratory, a handsome new office building and 'casino' restaurant for the staff, and most of the old laboratories have been replaced by new ones and re-equipped.

At Zuffenhausen, too, the main plant looked different from one year to the next. In 1986 a modern paint plant was opened at Works II at a cost of DM100 million, and across the road a swathe of land, formerly a Porsche car park, was being transformed into a new DM125 million three-storey body plant. This is 132 metres

A scale model of Works V, 'the last of the biggies,' says Peter Schutz of the modernization programme. All six and eight-cylinder body assemblies are to be transferred to this ultra-modern plant during 1988.

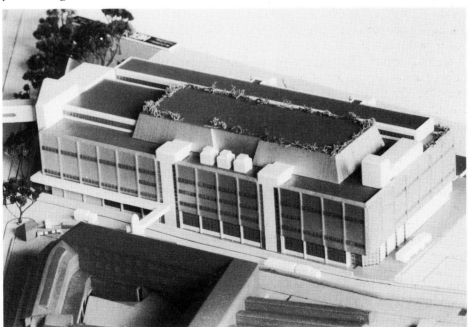

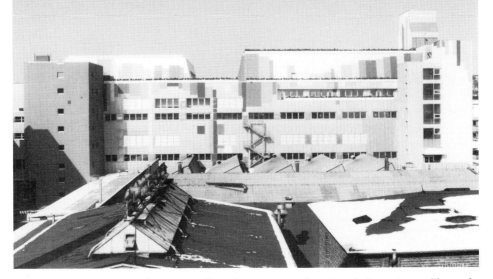

Opened in 1986 at a cost of DM100 million, the new paint shop dwarfs the antiquated barracks housing the 911 assembly lines. These will be dismantled in 1988/89.

in length, will be more automated than the existing 928 line, and will raise production capacity by a further 20 per cent to 120 cars per day.

On two-shift working Porsche will, therefore, be capable of building nearly 23,000 911s each year, half as many again as in the halcyon days of the 1960s . . . and that will be 25 years after the 911's first public showing! There is no doubt that Professor Ferry Porsche, described by his son Wolfgang as 'a man of vision' was right about the 911 all along. In his 78th year, as this text is prepared, Professor Porsche attends his office in Works I most mornings of the week, and Dr Wolfgang Porsche, his youngest son, frequently deputizes for him at official gatherings. Young Dr Porsche resigned his job at Daimler-Benz in 1981 to set up a 'small, unofficial office' next to his father's, and is one of three members of the family on the Supervisory Board.

There were people, early in the 1970s, who believed that only the largest manufacturers would survive future economic downturns. Insofar as mass manufacturers are concerned they may have been right, in that interdependence is continually increasing in components, and smaller companies are merged with larger ones. In the specialist fields, however, companies such as Porsche, Jaguar and Aston Martin have survived, with varying degrees of ease, to become leaner, fitter and more profitable. Peter Schutz's basic philosophy that the market for specialized products would not only continue to exist but would expand has been borne out by experience. Expansion is easier for a small company than for a large one, but major capital expenditures needed to modernize and improve efficiency are not so easily found, and there is considerable pride at Porsche that the great sums invested in the past seven years have all been drawn from reserves, nothing borrowed.

When Peter Schutz eventually retires it is quite possible that he could write a best-selling 'How to' business textbook. A study of his words reveals much about the man, and his policies that have been shown to transform a prestigious, family-owned company with average commercial performance into one with a business record to match its exploits on the race circuits.

Peter Schutz himself said, 'I see my job as getting the best people into this company, doing what I can do to organize the task so that these people have the freedom to perform to the best of their ability without encumbrance by bureaucracy and systems. You've got to have those in order to keep track of what's going on in the business, but you have to be careful that you don't frustrate people with bureaucracy. Then, having put them in a position where they're free to perform, they have to be motivated to perform to the best of their ability. In my view that's the job of a chief executive.

'Any team reflects very diverse viewpoints, which gives rise to a great deal of conflict of views and ideas, and my job is to manage that conflict, to set a course for the company both strategically and tactically. Strategy is what we need to do, and why we need to do it. Tactics concentrates on the "how" and the "who". I have to see to it that these things happen.

'My job is not as an engineer, nor as marketing, nor as finance, nor as personnel, nor as manufacturing, but it is all of these things. I have the task of a general, and you wouldn't ask him if he's going to see to it that the aeroplanes fly, that the tanks roll . . . he has people to see to those things.

'In my view you have only two options: do the job yourself, and get everyone to help you, which is one concept, or get the people together and motivate them, get *them* to perform. But, once you get a group of more than 20 or 30 people there really is no option. I know some people who can work that first option with 120, or 130 people; they are very strong entrepreneurs, the paternal genius, but there are very few people who can operate in that way. Once they get beyond a certain size they almost inevitably lose control of the business.

'Of the future at Porsche, I would predict more of the same. More of what already is, and we don't have plans to make it anything else. We don't view ourselves as being in the sports car business at all, much as that may surprise you, we're in the entertainment business. We build high-tech entertainment articles that usually have the combustion engine in their middle point, and have to do with movement. We are developing an aircraft engine, and I'm also very excited about using that engine in a helicopter. We are working with a company that's making a boat engine out of the V8, and these are all activities that interest us at Porsche. They're all to do with moving from one place to another in a way that people enjoy. We supply people with things they feel they have earned, as the fruits of their labours. We have no plans at this point to build boats or planes, but that would be a logical extension of the business.

'Having a Porsche, more than any other type of car, is a hobby, one that can be enjoyed in the course of many other things. Driving to and from work; taking to the mountains for 45 minutes after lunch before getting back to work. People have more freedom, perhaps, to enjoy Porsches than their sailboats or aeroplanes, or holiday homes because those things *demand* leisure time. Our customers tend to be busy professional people who look for entertainment or hobbies that can fit easily into their schedules.

'Porsche is only vulnerable to one thing, in my view, and that's if people stop buying our products and services. As long as you have customers you can manage companies through almost any circumstances. And if, because of the dollar or whatever else, companies start going broke we will certainly not be among the first. Along with the dollar, interest rates have fallen dramatically.

'Owning a Porsche consists of three elements: the cost of money, the cost of depreciation, and the cost of insuring the thing. Insurance costs are escalating incredibly. But if the interest rate on money you have invested in a Porsche, or a vacation home, drops then the cost of owning these things drops. If at the same time they retain their value in a realistic sense then the cost of owning them is realistic.

'In the past year we have raised our prices by 20 per cent or thereabouts, but since the American interest rates are 12 points lower than they were when the dollar was over three Marks the cost of owning a Porsche hasn't changed very much, and that's the reason why we can still sell them. Anybody who's smart enough to buy a Porsche has figured this out, or has an accountant to explain it to him. Our customers are not generally people who've arrived at this point easily. They don't throw their dollars, or pounds or D-Marks about. I don't believe that the American market is any more, or less price sensitive than any other. What really matters is value.

'Perception of value can be a problem. We are finding out today, I think the whole industry is finding out, that people are not willing to pay for four valves per cylinder. Several manufacturers, Mercedes, Volkswagen and now ourselves with the 944S, have brought four-valve technology to the market. We have a tough time selling it. It's expensive, and the customer just does not perceive that it's worth the extra cost. In the 928S-4 it has worked, but in that model we also increased the horsepower in the engine very significantly. There are many examples where you make significant advances but the customers will not pay unless there are clear benefits that can be demonstrated. The technology may be very exciting, but the benefits have to be clear and demonstrated.

'If you tell the world you've just gold-plated the flywheel, people are not going to pay for that. You may have put some value there, but if it's not quantifiable people won't pay for it. If it is, they will.

'I am sure that we may, from time to time, put developments into the cars that we think are great, but when you expose them to the market place the public puts a different value on them. In our company most of us under-estimated the impact of the 928S-4—I did myself, until I drove it. We saw all the things on paper, the new brakes, the new engine, the new acoustic treatment, the lower air resistance . . . the air resistance doesn't mean much until you've driven the 928 for hours on end at speed, perhaps into a 30 mph headwind, and then you stop for gas. And you find you've averaged better than 20 miles per gallon. All of a sudden new concepts, and features like thermal efficiency take on a new meaning, because you've experienced the benefit, and then the customer makes a decision, and customers don't make mistakes.

'The 928S-4 has become a very expensive car and none of us is very happy about the escalation in cost. But, if you put the kind of technology into the car that allows it to do the things it does, that's expensive in terms of development and the components that go into the car. It is something that we give a lot of thought to, whether the features that we put in are going to be perceived as benefits by the customers. The market for the 928S-4 is greater than we can satisfy at the moment, so that is a justification, and we always consciously try to keep supply a little bit below demand.

'The dollar today (DM1.78 in January 1987) has caused us to take certain steps. If it stays at this level we will have to curtail some of our investments, which is all right because we have the biggest investments behind us at this point. You must remember also that there are two factors that mitigate. One is that we basically compete with other companies that have the same problems. In Japan there are manufacturers that compete with our four-cylinder cars while mostly in Germany, except for Jaguar in Great Britain, there are products that compete for the attention of our customers in the higher priced ranges. Certainly Japan and Germany have exactly the same problem, and as a result there is some opportunity to recover some of the deficit in pricing, because everybody has to do it.

'Beyond that, what we have done is sold more of our Weissach capacity instead of using it for our own purposes, and in that sense you can view the investment in the 959 as an investment in future technology. We were able to afford it at a time when the dollar was high. At today's level there isn't going to be another 959. But then there doesn't have to be, because we have made that investment and now we are busy integrating those developments into our production cars. Beyond that, we've had to make some economies internally, but this is do-able because we've been through a significant growth phase. In that sense it's a healthy development to go into a consolidation phase, and to comb through a lot of the things that happened in the growth phase and re-examine them.

'But we are not going back to the siege phase, that's certain. The ability to sell engineering is important because other companies might have to lay engineers off to economize; we don't have to do that, so what might be a cost column becomes a revenue column. I think we can continue to make a profit, and serve our customers, at the present exchange rates. I would say that no matter what level the dollar is at, we'd find a way to work with it. It has been as low as 1.72 in 1979 and as high as 3.40 in 1985, so it's not as though the dollar is making history today, it's merely at the bottom of its cycle. If you and I knew where the currencies are going tomorrow we wouldn't have to work!

'You ask me to sum up the past six years, and I'd say that this is a voluntary assignment. If anyone is in a job like this and doesn't want to be, he simply has to get up and leave. I am happy, since the job has exceeded all my possible expectations. That is not to say that every job does not have parts which are more fun than others, but I can't think of one which would be more exciting than this one. The best part is getting to know the customers—I have gotten to know the most exciting and interesting people in the whole world. They are people I would never have dreamed of meeting, except through this job.'

2

The Weissach Report

Larger manufacturers in the automotive field may have greater research and development facilities, but none would have more modern equipment than Porsche's at Weissach and none would have the diversity of skills. The 2,300 engineers and technicians at Weissach are organized in a matrix system with the heads of nine departments reporting to Professor Helmuth Bott, the director. These are Dipl Ing Paul Hensler (powertrains), Dr Wolfgang Eyb (chassis development), Anatole Lapine (styling), Dipl Ing Helmuth Flegl (research/advanced development), Peter Falk (competitions), Dr Reiner Fritz (chief engineer, outside orders), Klaus Grewing (military development), Horst Marchart (chief engineer, company developments) and Richard Hetmann (Porsche passenger car development).

Working within these departments are a number of engineering Professors and Doctors (or both, instancing Prof Dr Dusan Gruden, head of powerplant research), forming one of the greatest concentrations of engineering talent to be found anywhere in the world. Much of their work is cross-indexed so that Dipl Ing Hans Mezger, race engine designer, could pick any number of brains to solve a problem, or any departmental head could refer to Mezger for his advice. For the 120 outside customers the availability of such a diversity of skills can be irresistible, and Professor Bott is proud to claim that he has never lost a customer.

Peter Schutz points out that outside contracts are never solicited—clients come to Porsche. He, Professor Bott and Professor Dr Rudi Noppen (in charge of Zuffenhausen production plants) make it their business to know the heads and managers of client companies and to keep the relationships going at the highest levels; the average value of each outside contract is DM850,000 per annum, so some of the clients must be very big indeed.

For clients there are strong advantages to placing some development work outside. The in-house payroll can be kept to a predetermined level (important after two serious recessions in the past 12 years), specific one-off developments such as a new gearbox design can be completed, at a fixed price, by people whose job it is to carry out such assignments, and finally there may be new techniques that the client has yet to hear of. While research would remain confidential to the client, the engineers concerned would not be expected to 'unlearn' something important when moving on to the next contract.

Above *Porsche's showcase is the 148-acre Weissach research and development centre, which includes a multiple test track, the competitions department and, in the foreground, the design centre and test facilities. The 'hexagon' was completed in 1974 and the new administrative building, on its right, in 1986.*

Professor Helmuth Bott, director of research and development.

Dipl Ing Paul Hensler manages powertrain developments, and the test facilities.

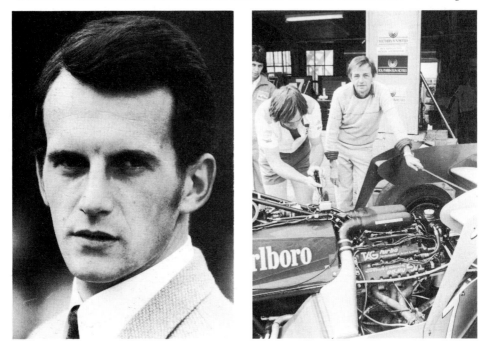

For these reasons Porsche regards its own passenger car range, and its own racing activities, as being supremely important in spreading the Porsche message around the world. Within the past six years the four- and eight-cylinder Porsche models have been brought close to perfection, as defined by engineering techniques in performance and thermal efficiency at the present time, and the 959 model exemplifies the range of possibilities available to the six-cylinder 911 range in the next decade. All models are constructed in galvanized steel, aluminium and composite materials and have a ten-year anti-corrosion warranty coupled with a two-year mechanical warranty, ensuring that their retained values remain high and that they represent good investments for business-minded customers.

By 1974 all research and development activities had been moved from Zuffenhausen to Weissach, a 'green field' site initially covering 34 hectares (84 acres) between the villages of Weissach, Flacht and Mönsheim. Nine hundred engineers and technicians were employed there on Porsche developments, but including DM10 million worth of contract work for Volkswagen and the German government. The takeover of the EA 425 contract did not cause any redundancies since the output was transferred to the in-house account, preparing the 924 model for production, but the staffing level remained fairly static until 1981 when 1,000 people were employed there.

Since 1981 there has been an explosion of activity as the total value of r & d business, including Porsche's own development, has risen from DM171 million to DM373 million, and of the latter figure DM100 million was actual revenue from clients; since 1981, the payroll has risen from 1,000 to 2,300 and,

Far left *Dipl Ing Helmuth Flegl has the key job of managing research and advanced development, his current projects including PDK transmission.*

Left *Dipl Ing Hans Mezger is chief designer of Porsche's racing engines, including in the past 20 years the 917, the 935, the 956, the 'Indy' units and the TAG Formula 1 V6.*

Right *Dipl Ing Norbert Singer has been competitions manager and car project leader since 1963. With director Peter Falk he has supervised seven sports car World Championship successes and is currently involved in the new CART single-seater programme.*

as Professor Bott points out, 40 per cent of the activity is on behalf of clients.

As already mentioned nearly all the contract work is carried out on a confidential basis, but the variety of cars to be seen in the workshops and running on the demanding test track represents a good cross-section of the industry's output. An infield military test ground, where rally cars are also developed, is regularly visited by two of Porsche's own developments, the Leopard tank and the Weasel half-track scout car. 'Some are small orders and in different fields, and we design not only cars, engines and gearboxes, but also motorcycles, and things like ORBIT and SAVE' says Professor Bott.

ORBIT and SAVE are two of the less glamorous projects undertaken on behalf of a government research department, involving modular cells for fire-fighting and ambulance rescue units. Professor Bott recalls, 'We were invited to look for new solutions to old problems in the fields of safety and rescue, and many elements that we proposed have been absorbed into practical vehicles today. The modular cabin is standard now with self-contained boxes for fire-fighting equipment, for chemicals, for people, and the results of our research were well received.'

Today Weissach covers 148 acres (60 hectares) still with room for further expansion, though a new parcel of land is purely for contingencies. The massive updating that has taken place since 1981 has been largely funded by profits from American operations and, as Mr Schutz says, the programme is now largely completed. 'At the time of the high dollar we re-equipped Weissach with a new wind tunnel, a new environmental centre, a new crash test facility, engine test facilities with modern dynamometers and instrumentation; there is hardly a part of Weissach

Left *Porsche has been involved with NATO designs since the war, and a leading project has been the design and development of the Leopard tank, tested at Weissach.*

Inset left *The Weasel armoured personnel carrier (APC) is another Porsche military design.*

Right and below *Modular designs for fire-fighting and rescue services were developed by Porsche for the German government in the 1970s, and have been widely adopted.*

that has not been re-equipped and modernized, which was absolutely the key to staying at the forefront of technology.'

While all European motor manufacturers have faced the same problems in developing catalyzed engines suitable for the American market, Porsche's programme has faced a particular hurdle since customers would not accept inferior performance. Professor Bott said, 'Porsche customers always want the most powerful car available and, especially the customers outside Germany, are not so interested in the catalyst equipment.

'We learned a lesson in 1974 when we replaced the 911 Carrera 2.7, with 210 horsepower, with a less powerful model. A lot of customers wouldn't buy the new model, and kept their cars or bought used ones with a few miles. When faced with the problem of introducing catalyst equipment therefore we knew that it would have to be more powerful than the model without a catalyst.

'Our solution was to introduce four-valve engines. The 928S developed 310 bhp with two valves and without a catalyst. The 928S-4 has a larger capacity, 5-litres, and develops 320 bhp with a catalyst offering better high-speed acceleration, better aerodynamics, and better consumption too. As you can imagine it was not easy to achieve these goals. With the four-cylinder engines we decided to keep the two-valve engine for the 924S and introduce the four-valve 944S with higher power than the 944, even with a catalyst. Later we decided to keep the two-valve 944 in order to keep the price down, nearer to the old model.'

The introduction of the 959, developing 430 bhp with catalytic equipment, was a particularly hard task due to the short exhaust system length and the difficulty of installing the sophisticated three-way Lambda probe. Ironically only about four of the 200 production cars were so equipped. Production of the 200 customer cars was delayed by around 18 months for various reasons, the main one being the requirement to equip this 'showcase' model with a catalyst, and although the decision was taken in 1985 not to offer the 959 in America the research continued. As Dipl Ing Paul Hensler points out, 'To meet all the US regulations we would need to reshape the car completely, and we decided to incorporate the technology into future generations of the 911 instead. But these days you cannot develop an expensive and sophisticated model without a catalyst, and the new European regulations demanded this. That greatly increased the development time, and we have now found that only three or four German customers wish to have the catalyst version. For us, it's not a question of how many people want a catalyst. . . rather, a demonstration that we can do it!'

While the main thrust of development in the past three years has concentrated on combining low-pollution solutions with ever higher performance, there are other requirements which occupy the minds of Professor Bott's staff at the present time: inflatable air bags on the steering column to increase safety in the American market, and lower noise. In the latter area the Swiss government is leading the way, and others are expected to follow.

'The air bags were shelved for a long time in America, because it was believed that if 75 per cent of the population wore seat belts then the air bag solution wouldn't become mandatory,' said Professor Bott. 'Then they changed the rules and said that air bags would become compulsory even if 100 per cent of the population wore seat belts. That involved us in a great deal of work, as much as anything in making changes to the bodies. In order to inflate the air bag in front of the driver and passenger you must change the interior completely. That was the original reason for designing a new interior for the 944, and now we need a new interior for the 911. We had to crash a lot of cars, 90 last year, to test the air bag system.

'It's very expensive, of course, because you have to crash the latest cars even if the model change is just a facelift. We were very pleased to find that the older 911 models could pass the crash test even though they were not designed for it, despite having the fuel tank at the front, and we haven't needed to make any changes.'

Peter Schutz has his eloquent way of describing the work needed to reduce noise levels. 'Switzerland has just introduced new noise regulations, and we cannot sell the 911 Turbo right now. Some people's pleasure is sitting on their front porch enjoying the peace, without being inundated by noise. We go along with that. We are a society, the world is getting more crowded in places, and we all have to live together on this ball, called Earth, that's rolling through space!

'Maybe my invention will find a market one day. A few years back I had a 944 Turbo which was pretty quiet. So I had them tape a microphone under the bumper, and taped the exhaust noise through the hi-fi system. I had a volume control and whenever I wanted to I turned the radio off, turned up the volume, and I thought I was in a race car. I kept the windows closed and no-one knew how much fun I was having. I have not, however, been able to sell that idea to my colleagues. . . not as an option on a Porsche, anyway.'

Responsibility for achieving the goal rests with Professor Bott, though, and his description is more to the point: 'The solution available to most manufacturers who wish to sell cars in Switzerland is to reduce the power, but we do not want to do this. We do have to reduce the noise of the engine, and do other things to the car, but not reduce the power.

'The 911 has a particular problem because the exhaust system is close to the engine, and the noises are not separated. The noise is greater, for a shorter time, so we need to do a lot of development in the next three years. Several years ago we encapsulated the 911's engine but that adds about 60 pounds to the weight of the car, and adds a lot of expense, so this is not the solution that we are looking for.'

For a great many customers of course, the noise of a Porsche flat-six, or a Ferrari, is a principle attraction of buying the car. Would a Porsche that's no noisier than a family saloon still be attractive? Bott replies, 'Well a 911 will always be noisier because its engine is closer; if you put the engine in front it would seem less noisy, but this is partly an illusion. Really, it is better to make engines less noisy, especially if you're going to drive a long distance. We see this in the development of the PFM 3200 aircraft engine, which is 6-7 dB less noisy. We believe that this is wonderful! It sets a new standard for aircraft engines, because so much can be achieved with the muffler. Our Mooney has a noise level of 61 dB, when the regulations allow 78 dB, and that was very welcome to the crew who flew one around the world.'

_____Electronic advances_____

Micro-computer technology has been the single most important advance of the 1980s, making possible the sophisticated Motronic engine management system first seen on the 944 model in 1981 and enabling engineers to achieve the previously impossible equation of raising power while reducing emissions.

E-Prom is the Weissach buzz-word. It stands for 'Erasable Programmable Read-Only Memory' and, to the layman, is a micro-chip the size of a fingernail. Each E-Prom, though, carries 8,000 separate items of information to control the engine in all its possible phases. The ignition 'map' for instance carries 265 items of information, the fuel injection map another 265 instructions, and this microchip also controls turbo-charger boost, cold starting (with the complexities of cold starts in cold weather, hot starts in hot weather, and all combinations between), detonation control (so that the engines can run on almost any fuels, in any markets, with correct programming), and in the 928S-4 even controls the volume of air entering the engine compartment, by means of louvres in front of the radiator.

Dipl Ing Paul Hensler demonstrated a portable typewriter-sized programmer, into which an E-Prom micro-chip is plugged. Pressing a forward key takes the chip right through its range, as revealed on a screen, and at any point the operator can stop the program and change an instruction.

'For instance,' says Hensler, 'if you want to make an engine run 2 per cent richer for a 20°C cold start, that function can be changed in about two minutes.

'Before E-Prom technology came we would have had to enrich the engine mixture over a wide range, but now we can focus to an exact condition taking humidity, barometric pressure, temperature, even engine wear into consideration. You need the leanest possible cold start so as not to use too much fuel, or increase emissions. E-Prom does this for us, and checks all engine functions every 10-20 milliseconds.

'The E-Prom does enable us to get precise results, and programming is a fast process, but the new range of possibilities makes the tests rather lengthy. A chassis development programme in Sweden can take three months, optimizing the engine, suspension and brake systems on ice and snow, and in a variety of ambient conditions. We have to test all the philosophies such as ABS braking, slip control, ride height control and engine functions from minus 25°C to plus 40°C, which is another test programme of course. One major programme was to get the engine to idle below 1,000 rpm when cold, at minus 25°C. No-one wants an engine to race when it's cold.'

E-Prom technology was useful at Le Mans in 1986. Following Jo Gartner's fatal accident at four o'clock in the morning the pace cars came out, lowering the average speed of the cars by half at the coldest time of the night. The works Porsche driven by Derek Bell, Hans Stuck and Al Holbert went on to win the race, and Peter Schutz recalls a particular episode with some pride. 'When that accident happened a young woman, one of our engineers, sat down at the back of the pits with what looked like a typewriter. She re-programmed the fuel system for both our cars, to enrich the mixture a little bit and not run so close to the limit. When the cars came in to refuel they changed the microchip boards and away they went again, correctly programmed for the new conditions, running slowly at night.

'We have found that our Group C racing programme, which forces a high level of economy, has been an invaluable tool in the development of more economical engines for our road cars. The electronic systems were really pioneered on the race tracks, and I think that if you look at the specific fuel consumption that is achieved in our Group C cars, and in the TAG engine, we have achieved some amazing thermal efficiencies. Mr Hensler, Mr Mezger and Mr Schaeffer are all available for our full range of investigations, not just for racing engines. We don't have a rigid bureaucracy at Weissach, and people are not channelled into thinking that other things going on are not their business.'

Porsche was one of the last leaders in technology to introduce ABS braking, which became standard equipment on the 928S in 1982, and as was explained at the time the Weissach engineers were not entirely happy with the 'first generation' systems. They worked closely with the Robert Bosch company in Stuttgart, as they did with electronic engine management, and with the tyre pressure warning system first seen on Porsche's racing cars at Le Mans in 1980, and now standard equipment on the 959. PDK (Porsche Doppel-Kupplung) twin-clutch semi-automatic transmission is another development, pioneered early in the 1970s but set aside for a decade until the suitable electronic controls could be developed.

In practice Porsche has five E-Prom programmes for each model sold in world markets, taking different prevailing conditions into account. Special programmes are needed for Australia for instance which, although a small market for Porsche,

Porsche Doppel-Kupplung (PDK) semi-automatic transmission has been tested successfully on the race tracks, and could be featured in road cars, at the earliest in 1991. It has two clutches, one of which is always engaged, and electronic shifting control.

needs its own programme to cater for 91-octane lead-free fuel. America and Japan have similar programmes for super unleaded fuel at 95-octane, while most European countries still permit lead additives in varying amounts. The days of altering the mechanical specifications of engines seem to be gone, though, certainly so far as Porsche is concerned. When turbo-charged engines came to the fore in Grand Prix racing, around 1979, Keith Duckworth dismissively called this 'screwdriver tuning' (though he had to follow this line of development himself, without option). Now, even the screwdriver has been thrown away. . . whatever characteristic is required of an engine can be achieved simply by changing the microchip board, and in future electronics engineers will achieve far better results in tuning than established 'old-fashioned' performance engine developers.

While the decision of 1979/80 to contest the Le Mans 24-Hour race with a factory team of 924 Carrera GTR models is looked back upon as a terrible mistake (apart from the ethics of leaving race-winning cars at home, the engines weren't terribly good, and Porsche's own 944 was but a year away), racing production line products does have a place in Porsche's programme. In 1986 the factory supported an extremely successful, and crowd-pleasing series of races for the 944 Turbo model, with catalytic equipment. The series was won by Joachim Winkelhock, younger brother of Manfred Winkelhock, the driver killed in a Porsche 956 at Mosport in 1985.

For the series, which looks like becoming a regular feature outside Germany as well, the 944 Turbo's engine was left alone at its production level of 220 bhp. Since the power is the same with or without catalytic equipment, it made sense to run the cars with this equipment installed, as proof of technology, since Germany, Switzerland and Austria are much more environmentally aware than other European countries at the present time. So equipped, the cars are capable of accelerating from the start-line to 100 km/h in six seconds and have a top speed of 152 mph (245 km/h) which is quite fast enough to guarantee a good competition. At the Norisring in 1986, in fact, the racing was so close that hardly any cars finished without major damage, but 80,000 spectators certainly had their money's worth.

Powertrain development

The decision was taken in 1983 to concentrate all Porsche engine development on the requirement for unleaded fuels, and to achieve identical engine performance for all markets regardless of catalytic additions, when it became clear that Germany would take the lead in Europe. Until the 1980s low emissions were a particular goal for the American and Japanese markets but the destruction of large tracts of forests, together with the emergence of the Greens as a political party, was having a major impact on public opinion in the Germanic mid-European countries. That car exhaust systems are responsible for 'acid rain', or even make a significant contribution, is a matter for debate, but any motor manufacturer who ignored the problem would be running against the tide of public feelings, and none could afford to do that.

In conversation Paul Hensler asked, rather pointedly, why the British seem to be uninterested in pollution control. . . even the engineers who face the problems have feelings about it. The explanation that Britain is surrounded by water, has no discernible acid rain problem of its own, and no Green movement that needs to be heeded, did not altogether satisfy him. The strength of feeling against the isolation shared by Britain, France and Italy, and felt by the Scandinavians too, is under-estimated by Britons who stand accused of exporting their environmental pollution, and this is a strong issue.

Recognition of the problem forced Porsche to turn to four-valve solutions, expensive but necessary. Until recently many manufacturers used four-valve technology as an efficient way of extracting more power from a given engine; the Japanese, lovers of technology, have done this for some years, and Porsche themselves came to four-valve technology in 1978 when the 935 and 936 racing cars needed more power and the heavy pair of valves incorporated in the air-cooled engine were no longer capable of fruitful development.

The switching to four-valve heads on the 935/78 and 936 engines involved water-cooling for the heads, and the system on the flat-six has been developed progressively in the 956 and 962C racing cars. In 1986, in fact, the production-based flat-six was converted to full water-cooling, finally dispensing with the big air fan. To some people this might sound like a heresy, but it was a necessary and logical step in the path of development since future 911 production engines may, indeed, need to be water-jacketed in order to reduce noise levels; the heating system, incidentally, can be much improved at the same time.

In order to see what Porsche may do in the future, a close inspection of current racing cars will provide a clue (PDK transmission is another example).

Four-valve cylinder heads offer all the possibilities needed for the future, especially in the fields of low emissions and higher power outputs. Paul Hensler believes, 'Four-valve cylinder heads meet today's goals better, in low-emission combustion and a higher degree of efficiency, plus best possible torque in all rev ranges. Once the combustion chamber possibilities of a two-valve engine had been exhausted we turned to four valves. This permits a central plug position with very short flame travel to all sides, so that the fuel is burned better and more evenly. You obtain good torque in the lower rev range and still have very good filling in the upper ranges. However, very high revs are not utilized in production engines since increasingly severe noise-emission regulations work against this.

'Four-valve technology with a nearly symmetric, roof-shaped combustion chamber allows higher compression for a given fuel, or allows the use of unleaded super of 95 octane instead of leaded super of 98 octane, with the same compression ratio.'

The development of the 2.5-litre 944S 16-valve and the 928S-4 32-valve engines is not coincidental, since the V8 is now almost exactly a pair of four-cylinder engines in 'vee' configuration. They have the same bore and stroke, identical cylinder heads, hydraulically lifted valves, camshafts, pistons and so on, leading to considerable economies of production. The two-valve engines in the 924S and the 944 are retained only for reasons of expense, to offer Porsche models at affordable prices, and it is evident that the 911 will also become a water-cooled 24-valve engined model in the not-too-distant future. The 959, its technical forerunner, already employs the 956/962 engine layout with four water-cooled valves per cylinder, with a capacity of 2,850 cc, and develops 450 bhp in production form, so it is potentially the fastest of all supercars.

Development of the 944S/928S-4 engine layout did not present any great technical problems. A short chain across the centre of the cylinder head drives the intake valve camshaft, keeping torsional vibrations as low as possible. The four-valve engines achieve very low specific consumption under high part-load conditions (coming close to diesel consumption) and allow the use of slightly 'longer' gear ratios which further improve the economy. Mechanical losses impair consumption at idle and in low partial-load conditions, but four-valve heads still provide higher efficiency at higher engine speeds.

In practical terms the 944S is very superior when catalytic equipment is installed, though without this equipment the advantages have proved less obvious to customers. In the 1988 model year, the 924S and the 944 shared the 8-valve engine rated at 160 bhp, with or without catalytic equipment—the 924S's power was raised from 150 bhp, the 944's reduced slightly from 163 bhp, although it had previously developed only 150 bhp with emission equipment. The 16-valve 944S is offered with 190 bhp whether or not it has catalytic equipment, while the 944 Turbo produces 220 bhp with or without catalytic equipment. There is only one model missing, it seems, and that is the 16-valve 944 Turbo which previewed the new range at Le Mans in 1981 (it developed 420 bhp and finished in seventh place overall). This Herr Hensler dismissed as too expensive, since considerable development would be needed to combine turbo-charging with the more bulky 16-valve head under the bonnet of a production car.

Although the 944S and 928S-4 share so many components they are 'tuned' (by micro-chips) in different ways. Hensler explains, 'For the four-cylinder engine, which already had good torque at lower revs in two-valve form, the target was a performance increase in the upper range—a "second spring" so to speak, which we appreciate in sporty, normally-aspirated engines. For the eight, which already offered excellent performance in the upper rev range, we increased torque considerably in the middle and lower rev ranges, particularly in consideration of the automatic gearbox. Four-valve technology, in conjunction with intake manifold layout and valve timing, offers us a means for altering performance relationships at will.'

One of the methods adopted for the 928S-4 in the realm of torque was a pronounced 'wave', or ram effect in the intake manifold system, and micro-chip tuning of the engine's characteristics when a higher gear is selected in the four-speed automatic gearbox. For smoother shifting the engine power is slightly reduced for half a second, avoiding the shock effect of a high-rev change, and an even more surprising effect is produced in the 944 Turbo engine. 'Turbo-lag' or the lack of turbo-charger boost is much less pronounced than it used to be, but may still be noticed if, for instance, the engine is run at light throttle/low boost and is then required to give full power for overtaking. In this situation the engine is allowed to 'overboost' at 0.9 bar (12.7 lb) instead of 0.8 bar (11.3 lb) for ten seconds, giving a useful 20 bhp bonus until the overtaking manoeuvre is completed.

Details of engine developments, model by model, will be discussed in the appropriate chapters, while this over-view has given some indication of the exciting possibilities opened by electronics in the past decade, and the general emphasis given to emission improvements and four-valve technology.

In 1969 there were 100 people working purely on engine development (there was a separate department for transmissions), but now Herr Hensler has 195 people reporting to him on engine development and 55 on transmissions, a total of 250; in addition he has responsibility for all the facilities within the area, including design, development, testing, certification, planning, maintenance, wind tunnel, emission control and environment laboratory, as well as engine and transmission test stands. The general manager of these facilities is long-time Porsche employee and former racing driver Herbert Linge, who also co-ordinates circuit safety measures at a number of German tracks.

Accepting that powertrain development is the single most important aspect of Porsche's development path, Herr Hensler must therefore be regarded as the second most senior engineer at the facility. As Professor Bott says, 'Many manufacturers, some of them our rivals, are able to produce new models every four or five years, and to incorporate the newest technology. Because of our low production we cannot afford to do this; we have to get a long life, 15 or 20 years at least, from each of our models, and therefore we have to introduce new developments, higher power and so on, quite frequently to keep the models interesting.'

Transmission development is always less spectacular, and tends not to merit the same attention as power units. The four-cylinder cars have five-speed transmissions supplied by Audi, a carry-over from the introduction of the 924 model in 1975. The 924 Turbo model featured an adapted Porsche 911 five-speed transmission which was more suitable for the power and torque (this gearbox was available optionally on the 924 for two years), but in 1979 Audi produced a new, uprated five-speed gearbox which has been adequate for every model up to, and including the 944 Turbo. For the 944S and Turbo applications, Porsche specifies a stronger crownwheel-pinion and closer ratios, but that is all. Audi also supplies the automatic transmissions available for the normally-aspirated four-cylinder models.

The five-speed manual transmissions fitted to the 911 and 928 models (and the four-speed gearbox in the 911 Turbo) are designed by Porsche but are built by Zahnrad Werk Neuenstein (ZWN), a Getrag subsidiary, which also makes the stronger crownwheel-pinion set for the 928S-4 automatic. The 928's four-speed automatic transmission, in other respects, is supplied by Daimler-Benz and is identical to that in the more powerful Mercedes automatics.

Porsche persisted with the Sportomatic gearbox for a number of years in the 911 model, offering an electric particle-operated clutch, but when the American market for which it was really intended showed no further interest it was discontinued in 1979, when an incremental power increase went beyond the Sportomatic's known capabilities.

The idea of an automatic or semi-automatic transmission was never dropped entirely though. The concept of a double clutch transmission, engaging an alternate set of ratios, was under development early in the 1970s but offered no real advantages at the time. In 1980 a 928 'concept car', the type 960, was shown in Frankfurt with a more advanced form of PDK (then called PDG), since electronic development was found to open a new range of possibilities.

PDK first appeared in a racing car at Kyalami, South Africa, at the end of the 1984 season and would appear quite frequently during 1985 and 1986. In 1986, in fact, it equipped the winning car in the World Championship Monza 360 kilometre race, and the car that finished second in the Silverstone 1,000 kilometres.

In principle PDK offers all the advantages of an automatic transmission, though with the control offered by a manual gearbox, and dispenses with the power-absorbing torque converter. . . It sounds ideal, and will be equally suitable for all models in the Porsche passenger car range though not, Herr Hensler says, before the 1991 model year at the earliest.

In charge of the PDK development is Dipl Ing Helmut Flegl, director of research at Weissach, who in earlier times developed the chassis of the 917 and its awesome successor, the 1,000 horsepower 917/30. He calls PDK 'a sporting automatic', and it can either be fully automatic, shifting ratios upwards and downwards according to the engine's speeds and loads, or driver-operated by means of push-buttons or a miniature lever.

Inside the gearbox is a pair of primary shafts, one bearing the first, third and fifth gears, the other second, fourth and, if required, sixth. Each has a hydraulically-operated clutch and, as one engages in response to an electronic signal, the other disengages. Shifting, therefore, is virtually instantaneous, and this is of great benefit on a race track when turbo-charger lag may become a factor.

In road trials, in Flegl's experimental 944, the PDK transmission has been shown to be up to 10 per cent more economical than a manual gearbox, and gearchanges are accomplished very quickly and easily. In racing cars, though, there was an attendant weight penalty of 77 lb (35 kg) compared with Porsche's rather heavy, synchronized five-speed racing gearbox, and that proved rather too much of a handicap on most circuits. Initially the PDK was unreliable in mechanical ways, giving trouble with clutch slip, fluid leaks and the selecting of two gears at the same time on a couple of occasions, but in 1986 the system was almost completely reliable.

Only at the Norisring in 1986, a championship race that Hans Stuck should have won (and thereby later become undisputed World Sports Car Champion driver), did the system let Porsche down when an electric terminal shook loose. 'It took ten minutes to find and ten seconds to fix' said Falk. In a fuel consumption dominated formula PDK was a rather heavy burden for the factory team, and would be used less often in 1987, except on circuits like the Norisring where its benefits outweighed the weight penalty. In the meantime, development concentrated on making PDK smaller and lighter, and in 1987 a 'second generation' PDK was seen to be 22 lb (10 kg) lighter, and very competitive on the track. Although Porsche withdrew from the World Championship midway through the 1987 season to concentrate on the CART programme, Stuck won the German Supercup series with a factory-prepared 962C PDK.

Gear changes can only be made sequentially, pulling the lever backwards with fingertip pressure for upward gear changes, and forward for downward changes. Stuck, the factory's race development driver, shows great confidence in the system. 'I have discovered one trick when I have a really tough man to outbrake. I pre-select second gear on the straight, still flat-out in fifth, knowing that it won't change until the speed drops enough to do that without over-revving. In the critical zone I can concentrate fully on braking, without heel-and-toeing and with both hands on the steering wheel. But you need a lot of practice and faith to time it right.

'Rain is interesting too. Nobody came close to my wet times in the Nürburgring training. The advantage was accelerating out of a corner in second or third gear, where you get wheel spin or even power oversteer and have to lift off or shift up, which also breaks the smooth power flow. With PDK you simply go up a gear and hold the drift. It's wonderful!'

A further development was tested in the 962 during 1986, and this was automatic downshifting. Clearly the production transmission has not yet been clearly defined, for Flegl says he prefers the driver-controlled mode, which is more sporting, while Hensler wants it to become a fully automatic, always keeping the car in the best gear for the prevailing conditions. 'It must be made smaller and lighter, as a priority,' says Hensler. 'We would also like to make it less expensive, because it involves two clutches, two hydraulic motors and systems, and switches and electronics which are new in the automotive industry.'

_____Weissach facilities_____

Of the 2,200 people working at Weissach, 1,000 are qualified engineers and the rest are mainly skilled mechanics and administrators. About 30 per cent of Porsche's employees, therefore, are involved in research and development, an exceptional figure in an industry that would normally allocate 6-7 per cent of its resources to future products. In fact about 100 engineers are involved purely in research, under Helmuth Flegl's management, and there are 800 specialists in the prototype build department alone.

The styling department, directed by Anatole (Tony) Lapine, accounts for 45 people and the competitions department, directed by Peter Falk, another 40 (ten engineers and 30 mechanics), which seemed hardly enough to cope with three main programmes in Group C World Sports Car Championship racing, the TAG Formula 1 engine and development of the type 2708 CART single-seater. Before major races, especially Le Mans, another 50-60 mechanics can be added to the strength drawn from nearby departments.

The test departments, under Paul Hensler's command, are the essence of Weissach, for practically every country has its individual requirements, some obligatory, and certification is a long and costly business; although Porsche has three main engine ranges of its own, there are roughly 50 variants for the world markets.

When Herr Hensler joined Porsche in 1958 all development work was carried out in a barrack building at Zuffenhausen, and remained there until 1971. A chassis dynamometer and elementary emission testing equipment was bought in 1968 when the Californians, concerned about their smog problems, talked of introducing basic emission standards (though that equipment is now in their museum) and with the move to Weissach the test department had four test stands, which was thought would be too many. As a matter of interest, Porsche was the first European manufacturer to receive California certification, born of necessity, since traditionally half the Porsches produced are exported to the States, and half of those are sold in California!

The original test stands were largely automated, outdoor rolling roads with cars purring along day and night, and automated equipment was used to operate

The new environment centre (MZU) was opened at Weissach in 1982, containing six highly sophisticated test stands able to monitor engine performances for all world markets.

A full range of climate control, even allowing for altitude, is programmed into the Porsche MZU test cells. Two hundred technicians carry out 4,000 tests each year.

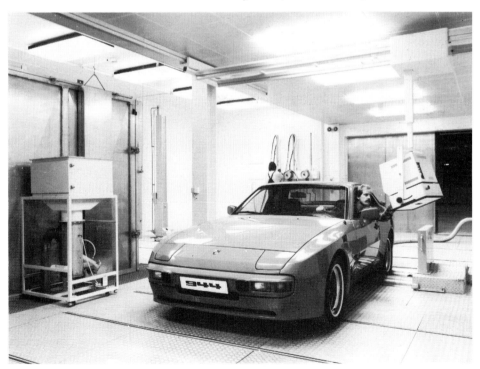

the clutch, gears and throttle, keeping to defined patterns in sequences lasting 50,000 miles. It needed just one man, to fill the fuel tanks at regular intervals, and involved no risks of bad weather or accidents interrupting the cycle.

The opening of the new MZU (Messzentrum für Umweltschutz) Environment Centre in 1982, with six advanced test stands, came not a moment too soon. It brought the whole operation indoors for a start, and made available a complete range of new possibilities for more accurate and more diverse measurements, altitude testing, engine knocking, extremes of heat and cold, consumption testing, even motor cycle testing.

Two hundred engineers and technicians were employed straight away to operate the equipment, and it is worth noting that while about 50 emission tests were carried out in 1971 for the American market, the number has now risen to around 4,000 annually, or 80 every week. The number of tests required for the States has steadied at around 2,000 to 2,500 per year in the past ten years, but as many again are now needed to meet various European regulations. At Weissach, as in all major research centres, there is a strong feeling that all European countries should work to the same standards for exhaust emissions and construction regulations, though that Utopia seems as far away as ever.

Without the environment centre Porsche could never have made such astonishing progress in catalytic development between 1983 and 1986, finding solutions which did not seem to be within reach in 1983 when the main topic of conversation at the Frankfurt Show was impending German regulations. The industry, realizing that some control was coming whether the engineers liked it or not, vociferously opposed the mandatory use of American-type catalysors which, they felt sure, would severely restrict the speed potential of their products.

Final proof that their fears were unfounded—or more accurately, that development would surpass expectations—came when Al Holbert drove a 928S-4 at over 171 mph on the Bonneville salt flats towards the end of 1986. Such performance was available not only in short bursts but in sustained high-speed cruising. Professor Bott says that the Lambda sond probe is the key, 'A wonderful system', together with new materials and construction techniques. 'With the pressures from outside to improve our engines, we have achieved results in the past three years that nobody could possibly have expected. The power to weight ratio, the power to fuel consumption and general performance levels are higher than could have been achieved ten years ago without catalysts. With 22 years of experience we knew how to find the solutions with three-way systems, and there is no longer any problem with power or with the lifetime of the system. Four-valve cylinder heads, with the spark plug in the centre, are another necessary step in improving combustion, and therefore lowering emissions, and our work now will concentrate on improving the fuel consumption.

'We are sure that the price of fuel will go up again, and we must be prepared to reduce the consumption to six or seven litres per 100 kilometres (40-47 mpg Imperial). Such a target seems almost impossible now, but so has everything that we've achieved in the past five years.'

Lighter vehicle weights and improved aerodynamics, together with higher overall gearing will also play a part in this equation, and a review of the 911 model's development over the past 20 years shows how this might be done. Performance has been improved dramatically without impairing the fuel consumption, but accepting that accelerations and top speeds need be increased very little in the next decade (though not reduced), further improvements will be measured in fuel efficiency.

Year	Model	Acceleration		Maximum	Overall
		0-60 mph	*0-100 mph*	*speed*	*mpg*
1965	911 2.0	8.7	24.1	130	21.1
1975	911 2.7	7.2	19.4	136	18.4
1975	911S 2.7	6.5	18.3	140	19.8
1975	911 Turbo	6.1	14.5	153	17.9
1985	911 Carrera 3.2	5.3	13.6	152	21.1
1985	911 Turbo 3.3	5.1	12.2	162	16.4

Figures from *Motor* or *Autocar* tests

In this time, power has increased from 130 bhp (911 2.0) to 231 bhp (911 Carrera 3.2) and to 300 bhp in the case of the Turbo 3.3, the latter model practically halving the time needed to reach 100 mph from standstill and offering incomparably better all-round performance, with a fuel consumption raised by 22 per cent. The Turbo customer would naturally trade off consumption for sheer performance, but the 450 bhp 959 model demonstrates further massive performance advantages without any deterioration in consumption. The basic concept of the 911, and particularly its bodyshell, has undergone no changes in this time, and in fact with far greater sophistication and comfort the kerb weight of the 911 has risen from 1,077 kg to 1,174 kg. In this light, Professor Bott's forecast for consumption does not seem far-fetched.

A completely new car design will spend 1,200 hours in the wind tunnel under development, and the value of this facility can be judged by the fact that the Cd (drag) factor for the 959 model is 0.31, compared with 0.385 for the 911 model. . . and lift has been reduced to zero, even though the bodyshell, the windscreen (and its angle) and doors are unchanged. The flatter headlamps, the carefully-blended body attachments and the integral rear wing all make their contribution to aerodynamic efficiency, and this has yielded performance in the case of the 959. In future, it could just as easily yield lower consumption figures without loss of average performance.

The full-size wind tunnel and the crash-safety research centre, both opened in 1986, are therefore extremely important developments, the last in the current series.

Before the wind tunnel was built a miniature version was constructed to accommodate 1:4 and 1:5 scale models, and continues to be in use. Other than minor variations the two tunnels are identical in design, since the scale version was built as a prototype. This logical step has immense value since clay models can be tested exhaustively without taking up valuable time in the big (and expensive) tunnel, which consumes 2,600 kW of power at its maximum setting.

The tunnel is 150 metres in length and 29.50 metres in maximum width, and in it cars can be tested at up to 230 km/h (143 mph) and at temperatures of up to 45°C. The chamber in which the car is positioned on a turntable has a new concept in slotted walls which allows an unusually high degree of accuracy in measurements, known as aeronautical flow quality, but it can also be adapted to the less accurate (but less time-consuming) 'free jet' system which is more usual in the automotive industry. The full-size tunnel, opened too late for the 959's final development, has nevertheless confirmed the accuracy of measurements in the scale-size tunnel, and is now being used extensively for development of the CART racing car and modifications to the 962/962C Group C cars.

While previously the crash-test procedures were somewhat rudimentary, the new laboratory enables Porsche to meet the highest standards (US 208, 212, 301 and so on). Head-on collisions at 50 kmph are routine, and the equipment facilitates angled impacts, side and rear collisions, and static compression tests on the front and rear body zones. Body element and structural profile analysis help determine body impact absorption and, of course, the photographic and

The new crash laboratory at Weissach enables Porsche to meet all world standards. All types of impact can be simulated, and the results recorded on film.

measuring processes are vastly improved. Clients who want major structural or styling improvements carried out on their products must first submit a car for detailed crash analysis in case extra work is needed in improving body strength.

There is hardly an aspect of vehicle design, construction, styling and development that is not among the range of services offered by Porsche's Weissach facility, including military developments, aero and marine engines, motor cycles, racing cars and competition engines. Professor Ferdinand Porsche, who founded his own company in 1931 as a consultancy for anything that moves on land, sea or in air, would approve of all that he might see today.

_____PFM 3200 aero engine_____

As long ago as 1908 Ferdinand Porsche, when technical director of Austro-Daimler, produced a power unit for the young airship industry and in the 1930s his consultancy firm designed a 32-cylinder rotary aircraft engine of 17.7 litres (Type 70) and a V16 aero engine of 19.7 litres (Type 72). Then in 1943 the diminutive Volkswagen flat-four air-cooled engine was used to power an aircraft to 84 mph (140 kmph), and in 1959 Porsche offered its own development, the type 678 which in various forms developed between 55 bhp and 75 bhp.

It was not surprising that Porsche proved co-operative when the British Aerospace Developments company suggested using a pair of 911 flat-six engines to power its new AD 500 airship, which made its maiden flight early in 1979. Maybe they were not very busy at the time, but Porsche's top engine designers Hanz Mezger and Valentin Schaeffer were assigned to this straightforward project; the engines were still able to develop their full 180 bhp for take-offs, and 120 bhp for cruising. Air-cooled engines are inherently satisfactory for aviation work, and the main development centred on dual ignition for safety, and regulating the Bosch fuel injection to work correctly at altitude.

The AD 500's maximum speed was quoted at 71 mph (114 km/h) and there were plans to substitute 300 bhp Turbo engines in this, or a larger development. The Aerospace Developments company then met financial difficulties and was later reformed as Airship Industries, backed by Colin Bond, the Australian magnate who captured the America's Cup in yachting.

In September 1983 the first of four new production airships, the Airship Industries Skyship 500, was test-flown with the latest 204 bhp version of the 911 engine, and since then the Skyship 600, larger and powered by a pair of Turbo engines each rated at 270 bhp, has been flown.

With enthusiastic backing from Peter Schutz a much more ambitious project was under way, and in the summer of 1984 the PFM 3200 aero engine received its airworthiness certificate. It finally went into production early in 1987, and a turbo-charged version is being developed, alongside another suitable for aerobatics.

Based on the 3.2-litre Carrera flat-six, the PFM engine develops 212 bhp at 5,300 rpm for take-off, and 200 bhp at 5,000 rpm for cruising. The engine has changed substantially in one respect, in that the camshafts are driven by gear

Left *Porsche's PFM 3200 aero engine is a successor to post-war designs of four-cylinder units. It is based on the 3.2-litre 911 Carrera six-cylinder power unit and has many advantages over conventional designs, especially in noise, consumption and efficiency.*

Below *Initial trials of the PFM 3200 engine were carried out in 1983, in a Mooney aircraft, and the certificate of airworthiness was granted the following year.*

Below *The Porsche 924, introduced in 1975, was in the Zuffenhausen company's range for ten years before it was replaced by the 924S model.*

Above *Porsche's own four-cylinder engine was installed in the 924 model in 1985, and the 924S immediately became more desirable.*

Above *Announced in 1981, immediately after a good workout at Le Mans, the 944 model became Porsche's highest-selling sports car.*

Below *The 924 Turbo gave the four-cylinder model a new lease of life, but Porsche regarded it only as a stopgap until the 944 range was launched.*

wheels instead of a chain, while the new housing carries two AC generators, vacuum and hydraulic pumps, the propellor governor and high tension distributors for the twin ignition. An entirely new design of propellor was designed for the PFM, more efficient because the inner portion does not have to pump cooling air to the engine (the fan is retained), and is capable of being reversed for short landings.

At 440 lb (200 kg) the PFM (Porsche Flug Motor) is the lightest of its type, as well as being the most economical with an average consumption of 13 litres per 100 kilometres (21.7 mpg) at 300 km/h (186 mph). This is achieved with commercial-grade leaded fuel, rather than Avgas, and the PFM is sold complete with a silencer which reduces the noise level to that of a Porsche 911, 61 dB, remarkably less than the permitted 78 dB.

A single lever controls the throttle, propellor and mixture regulation rather than three, making life far easier for the pilot, and Porsche looks for a useful portion of the market estimated at 200,000 aircraft in the 180 to 230 horse-power class.

To prove the engine, Porsche sent Michael Schultz and Hans Kampik on a round-the-world trip which started in July 1985 and ended in January 1986, the PFM engine installed in the company's Mooney aircraft. In six months they flew 62,000 miles (100,000 kilometres) in 600 hours, and completed 300 take-offs and landings without experiencing any problems.

_____Porsche dominant in racing_____

The fortunes of the Porsche company were at a low ebb in 1974/75, when we pick up the story, and so too was the competitions programme. The type 917 racing car had been an outstanding success, winning World Championships in 1970 and 1971, and the turbo-charged version had won Can-Am titles in 1972 and in 1973. Then the first oil crisis threw the world into turmoil. Car sales slumped disastrously and competitions, both races and rallies, were cancelled at an alarming rate in 1974.

Porsche pressed on with its planned development of the 911 Carrera RSR Turbo, a progression of the previous year's car powered by a 2,142 cc flat-six turbo-charged by the KKK system, and developing 500 horsepower. The Formula 1 engined Matras, Alfa Romeos, Gulf-Mirages and Lolas were lighter and much more aerodynamic, streets ahead in terms of absolute performance, but Porsche did well to finish second at Le Mans and second at Watkins Glen, eventually finishing third in the World Championship.

Victories, though, were not anticipated. The 1974 season was treated purely as development for the new Appendix J Group 5 'silhouette' formula, first expected to start in 1975, then postponed to 1976. This would write out the prototypes, substituting production-based racing cars bearing a resemblance to their forebears, and the intention of the FIA was to attract massive support from manufacturers such as Ford, General Motors and Toyota, as well as specialists like Porsche and BMW.

In a way Porsche's thorough preparation was a deterrent to others. The giants of the industry remained unimpressed, realizing that they'd need cars with Porsche levels of performance, and probably with turbo-chargers, on the mass production line even to contemplate rivalry. At BMW, Jochen Neerpasch also doubted whether he could compete, though an absolutely fearsome turbo-charged CSL Coupé was prepared for some races in 1976, and appeared in the hands of Ronnie Peterson and Gunnar Nilsson. It was awesomely fast, and led the Porsches on occasions, but destroyed gearboxes regularly.

The FIA and its FISA sport subsidiary realized at quite a late stage that the Group 5 'silhouette' formula might not be totally successful, and decided to continue the prototype breed as Group 6 with its own World Championship. The Group 5 and Group 6 cars would not run together, but as usual the Automobile Club de l'Ouest reserved its options and opened the Le Mans 24-Hours to all comers, thereby going outside the World Championship. That decision was totally justified when Renault announced a major bid for the World Sports Car Championship, and waged heady battles with Porsche in 1976, 1977 and 1978.

For the 1976 season Porsche prepared cars for three championships; the Group 4 934 model for the European Grand Touring Car Championship (all cars were sold to and run by customers), the Group 5 935, initially run only by the factory in the World Championship for Manufacturers, and the Group 6 936, largely based on the old 908 spaceframe design and run exclusively by the factory in the World Sports Car Championship.

The 1976 programme was undertaken mainly by Jacky Ickx and Jochen Mass, who almost two-handed beat Renault's sports car challenge at every encounter of the season. The Porsche 936 was powered by the 2,142 cc flat-six engine, turbo-charged and developing 520 bhp, while the Renault developed its 2-litre V6 racing, with four valves per cylinder and a Garrett turbo-charger, to produce 510 bhp.

There was little to choose between the Renault A442 and the Porsche 936 in terms of actual power and performance, but while the Porsche factory divided its effort between Group 5 and Group 6, always with Martini sponsorship, Renault should have taken the Sports Car Championship with ease. The French did not succeed, though, and were quite embarrassed at a series of driver and mechanical failures, and Porsche finished the season with two major titles (or three, including the European GT championship, where the Porsche 934 had no real opposition).

The Martini-Porsche driven by Jacky Ickx and Gijs van Lennep won the Le Mans 24-Hours at a canter after the Renaults dropped out, Porsche's third victory at the Sarthe and the first since 1971. The 935 model, contesting the World Championship for Manufacturers, did not have quite such an easy time since Porsche was forced to change the intercooler design, and this led to a mid-season bout of unreliability. BMW and the normally-aspirated 635 CSL drew threateningly close half-way through the series, but the Weissach engineers conquered the problem and drew away again.

The 934 was a straight development of the 911 Turbo, even having electrically-operated windows, and developed 485 bhp initially from the 3-litre engine. In order to compete in the 4-litre class (in which a super-charged or turbo-charged engine has its nominal capacity multiplied by 1.4) the 935 was basically a 2.8-litre design developing 590 bhp while the 936, as stated, ran a 2.1-litre version of the same power plant. Essentially, though, Porsche was running production or production-based equipment for both development and publicity purposes.

In 1977 Porsche withdrew from the World Sports Car Championship, as did Renault, both factories saving their big guns for another confrontation at Le Mans. (Alfa Romeo filled the breach, scoring runaway victories with the Alfa 33TT12 model in the Group 6 series, which had its 'world' title taken away at the end of the season.)

Giving full priority to the World Championship for Manufacturers, Porsche sold a number of 935 Group 5 cars to customers (notably Reinhold Joest, the Kremer brothers, Georg Loos and Max Moritz), these having newly-developed twin-turbo engines which were a little more powerful, at 630 bhp, and more responsive with a smaller turbo-charger on each bank.

Now there was hardly any opposition though, as BMW concentrated on the German championship, and on the 320i Turbo prepared in America by McLaren Engines. Suffice to say that Porsches won all nine rounds of the World Championship for Manufacturers, the factory winning four races and customers the other five. At Le Mans the Renaults faltered again, leaving victory to the Porsche 936 driven by Hurley Haywood, Jürgen Barth and Jacky Ickx.

This success, Porsche's fourth at Le Mans, did not come easily. The entry shared by Jacky Ickx and Henri Pescarolo retired with a broken connecting rod, so the Belgian swtiched to the Haywood/Barth car which had been delayed 21 minutes by a faulty fuel pump early in the race. That was quite a margin to give the four Renaults, but Ickx drove the race of his life, consistently under the lap record through the hours of darkness, and saw the lead for the first time on Sunday morning when the Renault driven by Derek Bell and Jean-Pierre Jabouille retired with engine failure. Even then, a holed piston 46 minutes from the end of the race threatened the leading Porsche, but it was so far ahead of the Renault powered Mirage of Vern Schuppan and Jean-Pierre Jarier that it was able to complete the victory at slow speed.

Not all of Porsche's developments are easy to anticipate and in 1977 a special version of the 935, the 'Baby', was to take part in only two races. It was designed to run in the 2-litre class, and to break BMW's run of successes in the lower division of the German Championship, which threatened an overall Porsche victory.

The 'Baby' had the smallest capacity flat-six ever produced, the 71 mm bore and 60 mm stroke (both unique) giving a capacity of 1,425 cc; turbo-charged, and multiplied by 1.4, the FISA-rated capacity was 1,995 cc. The engine delivered an overwhelming 370 bhp at 8,000 rpm, and the weight of the 935 was painstakingly reduced from 2,114 lb (970 kg) (935/77) to a featherweight 1,584 lb (720 kg), easily the lightest 911 derivative ever constructed. All the panels were made as light as possible, including use of the new aramid composite materials coming on to the market, it did not need lights, and the oil and fuel tanks could be made much smaller for a couple of one-hour sprint races. Jacky Ickx drove it at the Norisring, where the complete lack of heat insulation got the better of him, and again in the supporting race for the German Grand Prix at the Hockenheimring. He won that by nearly a lap, and the 935/2.0 was despatched to Porsche's museum!

Not only did Porsche win the World Championship for Manufacturers without difficulty, but American customers won every round of the SCCA's Trans-Am Championship, and seven of 14 rounds of the IMSA Camel Grand Touring Championship, Peter Gregg and Hurley Haywood being the most successful drivers with victories also recorded by George Follmer, Danny Ongais and Ludwig Heimrath. In time the 935's successes waned in Europe and in the World Championship, but in the States it continued to win IMSA races with monotonous regularity, until eclipsed by another Porsche. . . the 962.

For the 1978 season Porsche left all major championships to the mercy of its customers, concentrating on a new development which would start a fresh career for the 911's flat-six. Even in the late '60s it had been appreciated that power was limited by the weight of two large valves per cylinder, and their resistance to high engine speeds, and an experimental four-valve version of the flat-eight 908 racing unit was tested, then shelved.

The next major step forward, in fact the development that brings us to the present day and points to the future, was the completion of four-valve heads for the 911 engine, water-cooled too, though the cylinder barrels remained air-cooled.

The power advantage was clear-cut; with a nominal capacity of 3,211 cc (4,494 cc with equivalency applied) the 935/78 engine produced a prodigious 750 bhp at 8,200 rpm, while the customer 935 cars were pegged at around 650 bhp, depending on how much boost pressure was applied.

With exactly the same development on the 936 engine, still at a nominal 2,142 cc in order to comply with the overall 3-litre limit, power rose from 540 bhp at 8,000 rpm to 580 bhp at 8,500 rpm. All would have been well, had not the power proved too much for the five-speed Porsche transmission.

More interesting in several respects was the factory's unique 935/78 Group 5 car, designed by project and team manager Norbert Singer to take the regulations to their absolute limit. The front and rear chassis sections were cut away, replaced by spaceframe constructions carrying entirely different suspension more akin to Formula 1 than the production torsion bar design. The gearbox was turned upside-down in order to lower the engine, and the entire floorpan was reduced in height. Covering the original centre-section body was a long, flowing panel design which bore only a passing resemblance to the original, and the 935/78 was dubbed 'Moby Dick'.

The car raced only three times. Its debut at Silverstone in May 1978 was a tour de force, since Ickx and Mass led the six-hour race from start to finish and won by a clear seven laps, establishing a new lap record at 125 mph. At Le Mans,

Above *Porsche's first 'Indy' project was laid low by USAC's political decision to change the rules, just as Danny Ongais prepared to test the car designed by engineers Flegl and Mezger in 1979/80.*

Below *Al Unser Senior drove the Porsche 2708 Indycar on its debut in the CART Championship race at Monterey in October 1987. The car retired early, but was regarded as 'getting mileage' before the 1988 season.*

in the hands of Rolf Stommelen and Manfred Schurti, it ran with the leaders in the first hour but later dropped back with an incurable misfire and finished eighth; as a finale it raced at Vallelunga, but retired minutes from the end to allow Bob Wollek and Henri Pescarolo to take the flag.

The design of the 935/78 was generally copied by Kremer and Joest in 1979, but the factory would never allow any customer access to the 24-valve engine, claiming without conviction that it was 'too complicated'. Rather, there was no capacity at Weissach to build a series of extremely expensive water-cooled engines, and any customer having one would have walked all over his rivals. Anyway, the air-cooled engines continued to give good service, eventually taken out to 3,124 cc and giving a minimum of 680 bhp, or as much as 750 bhp on qualifying boost.

A special version of the 24-valve engine was prepared for Indianapolis in 1970, but Porsche was badly wrong-footed by the USAC rule-makers, who seemed to have given the green light to an engine of 2,650 cc and developing 630 bhp at 9,000 rpm at a certain level of boost. Late in the day the permitted boost was reduced and the engine would have given no more than 550 bhp, so Porsche and its Interscope partner withdrew, with a lot of huffing and puffing, and threw a dust sheet over the methanol-fuelled design.

So much time, effort and money had been expended on the Indy project that Professor Fuhrmann might have been pleased to see the Weissach-developed 924 Carrera GTR models racing at Le Mans, but others felt that a golden opportunity to wheel out the race-winning 936s was being wasted, and so it proved. The 924s finished sixth, twelfth and thirteenth, rather inconspicuously, while the 24-Hour race was won by Jean-Pierre Jaussaud and Jean Rondeau, in the Rondeau-Ford constructed at Le Mans. It may not have been good for Porsche but it was the best possible result for the organizers, and a vast crowd went home happier than if Porsche had crushed the local hero.

With Peter Schutz appointed to captain the ship in January 1981 a new impetus reached Weissach, including the competitions department. All six-cylinder developments held in the pending file were pushed to the front, and in the case of the 936 this involved the immediate preparation of the Indy-based 2,650 cc engine (there was no longer a top limit of three litres for prototypes). Reverting to water/air-cooling and tuned for commercial fuel (the compression ratio was lowered from 9.0:1 to 7.0:1), the engine still delivered a healthy 620 bhp.

The defeat by Renault in 1978 was directly attributable to failures in the five-speed gearboxes which were unable to cope with 580 bhp for 24 hours, so as an expedient the old Can-Am four-speed box was resurrected for the 1981 race. Naturally enough it had widely-spaced ratios and wasn't ideal, but it was strong enough to carry Jacky Ickx and Derek Bell to a perfect victory, the car sponsored by Jules toiletries.

Immediately after the race, thoughts turned to the 1982 season when a new set of regulations would be introduced. Group C would be controlled by thermal efficiency rather than any arbitrary engine capacity limitation, and the cars

Above *The ultimate 936 was the model which Jacky Ickx and Derek Bell drove to victory at Le Mans in 1981. Its 2.6-litre flat-six engine was derived from the stillborn Indy power unit.*

Below *The new competitions centre at Weissach keeps 40 engineers and mechanics busy all the year round, with Group C and Formula 1 World Championship programmes. Peter Falk is the competitions director.*

Above *Debut race for the Rothmans-sponsored Porsche 956 was at Silverstone in May 1982, when Jacky Ickx and Derek Bell finished second to a Group 6 Lancia. They won the Group C class, and the 956 would continue to dominate its rivals.*

Below *Rivals quaked when the Rothmans-Porsche team commanded the Le Mans 24-Hours in 1982, the three cars finishing in first, second and third places.*

could use no more than 132 gallons (600 litres) of fuel per 620 miles (1,000 kilometres). This is just the sort of challenge enjoyed by Porsche, and the 2.65 litre engine was carefully tuned in collaboration with the Robert Bosch company, first with mechanical injection and, from 1983 onwards, with the full Motronic system.

The 956 model was the first sports car ever designed by Porsche as a full monocoque, the design credited to Horst Reitter, and it also benefited from the 'ground effect' system, or under-car venturi, fashionable in Formula 1. It seemed a great step into the unknown, but to the team's everlasting credit it was absolutely right the first time out. The debut, at Silverstone, saw the 956 driven by Ickx and Bell beaten by the lighter Group 6 Lancia-Martini, ineligible for Group C points of course. The Porsche was dramatically slowing towards the end, out of fuel, since this was a six-hour race, and covered in excess of 1,100 kilometres, but in the proper 1,000 km races it consistently beat the Lancia and enabled Ickx to become the World Champion Group C driver.

Once again it seemed that Porsche's preparation, which would lead to over-whelming success, had deterred any possible opposition. Newly-appointed by Ford as director of motor sport, Stuart Turner cancelled the C-100 project at the end of 1982, and the Lancia LC2/83 became the only realistic challenger, though it did not beat the might of Rothmans-Porsche until September 1985!

The successes of the 956 and its 962C replacement are too numerous to

At the close of the 1982 season Porsche gained revenge on Lancia, the 956 driven by Ickx and Bell finished less than five seconds ahead of the Italian car. Ickx became the World Sports Car Champion for the first time.

Customer versions of the 956 enjoyed success and this one, 956/117 run by Reinhold Joest, won the Le Mans 24-Hours in 1984 and again in 1985.

recount in full. Suffice it to say that between 1982 and 1985 Rothmans-Porsche, or customers on occasions, established a legendary and overwhelming superiority over every rival. When the first customer cars were delivered in 1983 Reinhold Joest shocked the factory team with a victory at Monza, Thierry Boutsen and Bob Wollek neatly judging their fuel consumption to perfection, and later that season John Fitzpatrick's 956 again up-ended the factory, Derek Warwick starring in a rainy race and helped by Goodyear tyres.

More FISA dallying with the rules (threatening not to implement a reduction in fuel allocation, for which Porsche and Lancia had worked hard) caused Rothmans and Porsche to withdraw from Le Mans in 1984, and the race was won beautifully by Klaus Ludwig and Henri Pescarolo, in the Joest Racing Porsche 956. Were they lucky? The answer was found in 1985 when the Joest Porsche won again, this time driven by Ludwig with Paolo Barilla and 'John Winter' (Louis Krages), soundly beating the works Porsches!

The cigarette battle warmed up in 1986 when Jaguar and the Silk Cut brand challenged Rothmans-Porsche and won the second race of the season at Silverstone. It was an excellent success, but the factory Porsches were off form most of the season, running the experimental PDK gearboxes. These were heavy and still not quite reliable, and made the works team look rather ordinary on occasions. Not, though, at Le Mans, where two of the three Rothmans-Porsches had normal five-speed transmissions and one of them, driven by Derek Bell, Hans Stuck and Al Holbert routinely recorded the firm's eleventh outright success at the Sarthe. Also at Le Mans, on its track debut, was the type 961 development of the four-wheel drive 911, which will be discussed in a later chapter.

The type 962, a development of the 956 with the front wheels set 4.5 inches (11.4 cm) further forward in the chassis, earned an equally formidable reputation in America, in the IMSA Camel GT Championship. The IMSA organization fundamentally renounced the fuel efficiency controlled Group C World Championship but followed a parallel course for similar cars with weights related to engine size, and banning four-valve heads and twin turbo-chargers. The IMSA specification 962s therefore are powered by single-turbo, fully air-cooled Porsche engines not unlike those that powered the 935 in 1976. Chevrolet, Buick, Nissan and Ford all produced engines which might develop more power for qualifying, and occasionally beat the 962s in short races, but rarely had their measure in endurance events, Porsche's forte.

Porsche's reputation for excellent performance and reliability started at Le Mans in 1951, and regular victories began to pile up in 1968, when the 908 model proved to be the right one for the formula that prevailed. Except for occasional lapses when Porsche's management was preoccupied, the Stuttgart company has been in the limelight ever since, the result, I believe, of a total commitment to sports car racing.

In Stuttgart and Weissach, racing is Porsche's way of life, an exercise that transcends publicity or financial returns, and it would need a manufacturer with similar commitment to become as successful.

Porsche's doubts about concentrating on Group C were evidently dispelled in December 1986, and a month later Professor Bott expressed a commitment to the World Sports Car Championship. 'As long as there is a hard competition, I think we have to stay in Group C. We want to pursue new activities in different fields, but in Group C we are reaching the point where our customers cannot do any more development.

'Maybe our next step is to build a new car, because the 962 is five years old. It is impossible for us to think of Porsche not being involved in motor sports activities. In 1980 we were driving only to finish in tenth or eleventh places, and there were only a few customers who could understand our strategy.

'The 944 Turbo is a good solution because we can go to the races with our catalysts, a full muffler system, and show that our road cars are good on the tracks. I believe we need to have both programmes in fact. The TAG development was an outside contract, and at the same time we learned a lot; there is considerable overlap.

'It would be tempting for us to stop our Group C programme and concentrate on Indy cars, but we think our customers in Europe would not understand if we pulled out of the World Sports Car Championship. If you build customer cars they are still Porsches, and if they are beaten, Porsches are beaten. So we have to continue the devlopment, and we have to beat the competition.

'It is not enough to say that we have a new car with more horsepower, and better road-holding—we have to show them that it is one or two seconds faster. That is why we will continue to be involved.'

Mounting competition came from the Jaguar team, operated in Britain by Tom Walkinshaw. The developed XJR-8 version was given its debut in the two Spanish opening rounds, and won both of them, and the score was Jaguar — 4, Porsche — 0 when the teams went to Le Mans. That was a different story, for although Porsche was soon reduced to one good car, Bell, Stuck and Holbert kept pace with the three Jaguars and took advantage of various retirements and mechanical problems. At the finish Porsche gained its _twelfth_ victory, and Bell his fifth.

The Porsche factory then withdrew its team for the remainder of the season and Jaguar won the 1987 World Sports-Prototype Championship for Teams impressively, ending the five-year German supremacy in Group C. The Weissach engineers needed to concentrate exclusively on their new Indy car, and on the Formula 1 engine programme, and would then design a completely new Group C car, around the 'Indy' V8 engine, which was due to appear for the first time early in 1988.

Racing engines

Except for a brief period in the early 1960s when a special engine was developed for the type 804 Formula 1 car, which Dan Gurney drove to victory in the French Grand Prix in 1962, Porsche has largely stayed clear of single-seater racing. Sports cars, always, were closer to the products and even if they weren't powered by production engines (in the case of the 908 and 917) they were air-cooled and truly represented Porsche's philosophies.

It is in the nature of engineers, however, to explore boundaries and at Weissach there was always a body of opinion that leaned towards Formula 1, a tendency that Professor Porsche constantly kept in check. As one of the architects of the pre-war Auto Unions, and an enthusiastic test driver who might have developed a career in racing had his father permitted, his heart might have been in Grand Prix racing too, but his head ruled. 'Formula 1 racing is a circus, and the drivers enjoy more publicity than the constructors,' he said. When costs escalated, a company the size of Porsche would have been faced with a choice: single-seaters or sports cars. . . Ferrari chose single-seaters, Porsche chose sports cars.

It was always said that Porsche would become involved in Formula 1 if and when a team went to Weissach and in 1981 just such an approach was made by Ron Dennis, then an equal partner with Teddy Mayer in McLaren Racing.

Porsche had had its fingers burned with the abortive CART/Indy project in 1980, reinforcing its doubts about direct involvement, but the opportunity to design, construct and develop a Formula 1 engine at a client's expense was heaven-sent. If that sounds like a 'Heads I win. . .' proposition, then consider Porsche in the same light as Keith Duckworth and Cosworth, whose business it is to construct racing engines on a commercial basis.

When Ron Dennis and Peter Schutz signed the Formula 1 engine contract on 12 October 1981, the client had little idea how he was to pay for it, and later confessed himself to be 'paranoid' about the subject! McLaren was and is heavily sponsored by Marlboro but the cigarette company was wary of going into a multi-million-dollar engine investment programme, and after tackling various major manufacturers to see if they would share the investment, Dennis reached an agreement with the Saudi Arabian Ojjeh family, whose TAG company was

The TAG Formula 1 engine, designed, developed and maintained by Porsche, powered McLarens to World Championships in 1984, 1985 and 1986.

then a prime sponsor of the rival Williams Formula 1 team. The agreement was for TAG to become the client of Porsche, to have its name on the engine, and to take a major interest in McLaren International, with considerable backing guaranteed by Marlboro.

Hans Mezger and his long-time assistant, Valentin Schaeffer, went to work very quickly in collaboration with McLaren designer John Barnard, who laid down a precise package specification, and in March 1983 an extremely compact V6 engine of 1.5-litre capacity was shown to the world's press at the Geneva Salon. It is true to say that Mezger already had clear ideas about such a power unit but it was designed and developed at breathtaking speed, having run on a test bed at Weissach exactly 11 months after the contract was signed.

An 80° included angle was chosen in order to achieve the best solution to balance, and to maximize the ground effect capabilities of the McLaren. The TTE-PO1 engine had a bore and stroke of 82 × 47.3 mm for a capacity of 1,499 cc and was forced-aspirated by a pair of KKK turbo-chargers, developing 700 bhp at 11,500 rpm. Unlike Renault, Ferrari, BMW and Honda, TAG and Porsche chose not to develop special engines for qualifying, and capable of over 1,000 horsepower for a few minutes, on the grounds that it would add at least 50 per cent to the budget. The TTE-PO1 V6 weighed merely 330 lb (150 kg) ready for installation and, with Bosch engine management, was to prove the finest package available within the complex framework of power, economy and reliability.

Six months after its first bench trial, the V6 began a grinding routine of testing,

Though not usually the most powerful engine for qualifying, the Porsche-designed TAG F1 V6 proved the best power-economy package in race conditions over a three-year period.

4,000 miles (6,400 km) at Weissach, in a McLaren MP4/1D driven by Niki Lauda. Once again Porsche's own test track would be of immense value, though the pavé section which all Porsche's sports racing cars have to take in was excluded from the test routine.

The TAG engine was installed in Lauda's interim model MP4/1E for the Dutch Grand Prix, where it qualified nineteenth and retired with brake problems after an unspectacular run. Designer Barnard would have preferred to delay the debut until the specially designed MP4/2 was nearer completion, for the fact that the interim chassis had been designed for the normally-aspirated Ford Cosworth DFV V8 was clearly an embarrassment to the perfectionists, but at least the TAG engine had plenty of race miles in the latter part of the 1983 season without any major fundamental problems, and ran exceedingly well in third place at Kyalami, the last race of the season, until a complete electrical failure stopped Lauda abruptly.

For those who could read the writing, the story of 1984 was about to be written. John Watson was replaced by Alain Prost, whose time with Renault had come to an acrimonious end, and the Frenchman and Lauda proceeded to mop up the Grand Prix results. Eschewing a race-by-race summary, let me quote Maurice Hamilton, the Editor of *Autocourse*: 'It may have been tedious to watch Marlboro McLaren International win 12 races but the in-house competition and the drivers' reaction to it was fascinating. Prost was the quicker of the two but Lauda got there in the end and his achievement is made richer by defeating such

Above *Porsche's 'Indy' engine for 1987/88 draws heavily on development experience in Formula 1. This is a 90° V8 of 2.65-litres, rather than an 80° 1.5-litre V6. With a single turbo-charger the engine develops some 750 bhp.*

Below *Al Holbert, Porsche's North American competitions director, runs the most successful team in the IMSA series. His Löwenbräu-sponsored 962 won the Daytona 24-Hours in 1986 and in 1987.*

a worthy opponent.' Lauda took the title by just half a point, but in 1985 Prost was the dominant partner, improving from race to race, while Lauda suffered a number of uncharacteristic car and engine failures, and then retired from the sport for the second time.

In 1986 the Porsche-designed and maintained TAG engine was apparently eclipsed by the extremely powerful Honda V6 at the disposal of the Williams team, and Nigel Mansell seemed to be strolling to a world championship. Prost, though, was always lurking in the background, just a few points adrift, and seemingly came back from the dead at Adelaide to win the World Championship again, the first back-to-back driver's championship title since Jack Brabham's achievement in 1959 and 1960.

In the 1987 season Honda pulled out all the stops to win the World Championships, and the Williams and Lotus teams dominated the results. At least Alain Prost had the consolation of scoring his record-breaking twenty-eighth victory with TAG-Porsche power, before the V6 was withdrawn from service. The entire programme proved conclusively that Porsche wasn't *just* a big fish in the sports car world!

_____Back to Indy_____

There is no lack of continuity in Porsche's monoposto history. In 1962, when Dan Gurney won the French Grand Prix at the wheel of the Porsche 804, Helmuth Bott was the chief engineer, Hans Mezger the engine designer and current race director Peter Falk was a member of the management team. Mezger was also the designer of the flat-six Indy engine in 1979/80, and the TAG Formula 1 engine, so the pedigree of the new V8 is second to none.

The decision to return to America's premier series was inevitable, given the importance of the US market and Peter Schutz's own background. CART enjoys much better rule stability than USAC, and in Al Holbert Porsche has a North American Motorsports director who can manage the project in a professional manner. It was he who organized the sponsorship of the Quaker State oil company, long associated with his own Porsche 962 sports car team.

In choosing a 90° included angle for the V8 Mezger seems to have started with a clean sheet of paper, though visually and in many detailed ways the engine looks remarkably like the TAG unit, the castings for the crankcase being an obvious example. The V8, however, has a single large turbo-charger rather than a pair, and at 2.65-litre capacity produces over 700 bhp at the regulated 0.6 bar boost pressure. As is usual in CART racing the V8 runs on pure alcohol, which minimizes cooling needs.

Project 2708 was started in January 1986 and the engine ran for the first time on 11 December, within twelve months. The chassis is the design of Horst Reitter, designer of the 956 and 962, and the project manager is Norbert Singer who has managed the sports car team since 1973. Al Unser Senior drove the Porsche in the last CART events of the season, in readiness for a full season in 1988.

3

The four-cylinder ranges, 924 and 944

Porsche usually had a four-cylinder car in its range, starting with the 356 model (1948 to 1965) and the 912 version of the 911 (1965 to 1969). The 912 was not a very well-liked car, having the visual attributes of the 911 but the slower and noisier 1,600 cc engine, and it was dropped from the range when Volkswagen and Porsche set up a joint-stock company based at Ludwigsburg to market the 914.

The 914 was entirely a Porsche design, powered either by VW's four-cylinder engine (1,679 cc and 80 bhp) or by Porsche's 1,991 cc six-cylinder developing 110 bhp. In both cases the engine was mounted ahead of the rear wheels and the styling was rather boxy, an extreme departure from Porsche's usual rounded shapes. The 914 presented paradoxes; Porsche never liked it and discontinued the six-cylinder model after two years; Volkswagen kept production going, in Karmann's Osnabruck factory until 1975, yet initiated its replacement as early as 1971, Porsche's design staff then getting busy with the EA 425 project. While the 914 is not recalled with great affection in Europe, it sold very well in the States and some 115,000 were produced in total. It was not, therefore, the failure that many people believe.

One drawback of the 914 in Porsche's eyes was that it was a 'pure' two-seat design (conceived by Ferdinand 'Butzi' Porsche) outside of Porsche's traditional market. Volkswagen wanted its replacement to be a traditional two-plus-two, so Porsche started parallel lines of research into a new concept that would serve both the EA 425 and Projekt 928.

Fundamentally, air-cooling would be replaced by water-cooling, a basic premise that overturned the company's philosophy. Helmuth Bott had carried out an extensive evaluation programme in 1971, based on 40 criteria covering weight distribution and handling, emissions control, noise suppression, front and rear crash safety, interior space and comfort, even heater regulation, and he felt certain that a water-cooled engine would best meet the needs and requirements of what was left of the twentieth century.

Positioning the engine at the rear was ruled out on the grounds of handling (the Chevrolet Corvair, to which Porsche had contributed, had been heavily slated by Ralph Nader) and safety, especially in rear collisions. The options were

Left and middle left *In 1972/73 two utterly unremarkable cars, an Opel Manta and a BMW 2002 in less than pristine condition, served as test-beds for the Porsche-modified Audi engine and the new transaxle system.*

Below *Rather more curvaceous than the 924 production car, this prototype was undergoing trials early in 1974.*

Right *Installed in the Manta, the prototype 924 engine had a rough-looking 'bunch of bananas' induction manifold for the Bosch K-Jetronic system.*

narrowing and in October 1971—on his birthday in fact—Dr Fuhrmann signed a proposal to develop the 928 as a water-cooled, front engine model employing a trans-axle system, positioning the gearbox at the rear in order to achieve equal weight distribution.

Some years before, Dr Ferry Porsche had made an interesting comment: 'We are not bound by any concept, we are just bound to make any concept work better than others.' Volkswagen's order to develop the EA 425, which clearly would have a water-cooled engine at the front, provided the basis for a new design and development concept.

In 1972 and 1973 some rather unremarkable, unkempt cars were seen in the Stuttgart region. There was V1, a Mercedes 350 SL, original except for the trans-axle suspension system; and V2, an Opel Admiral with further suspension developments, while an Opel Manta and a BMW 2002 were used for research into the 924 concept.

An attractive two-plus-two coupé body shape was formed in Tony Lapine's styling studio, and photographs taken in 1974 show it to be very curvaceous, more Italian than German in styling, and a complete breakaway from the 914. By the end of that year the 'roundness' had been toned down, the rear quarters for instance being more vertical and continuing a 'waistline' right along the flank and round the back. The glass hatch at the back was larger with considerably more wrap-round, improving both the appearance and visibility, while at the front the bonnet line was continued forward to the fibreglass-insert, impact-absorbing bumper bar, straightening out the profile of the headlamp pods. As originally executed the

EA 425 might have had difficulty in standing the test of time, but the definitive 924 shape has been accepted universally.

When Porsche bought out VW's interest in the EA 425 in February 1985 it entailed raising DM100 million at a very awkward time, but as Professor Bott confirms it was always intended to have a four-cylinder model in the Stuttgart line-up, and if it had not been the 924 then Porsche would have needed to start from scratch. Mr Hensler has pointed out that there was a study on a four-cylinder version of the 911 engine, though such a unit was never actually built. Time and cost dictated acceptance of the 924, since to start again would require a minimum of five years in development and an investment of at least DM150 million. Really, there was no other way to go, for at that time it was supposed that the 911 had a maximum remaining useful life of five to seven years, and sooner or later a fresh model line would be needed.

The decision was sealed in February 1975 with production planned for 12 months hence, and in the meantime there was the question of American sales to be considered. The Karmann contract was running out (Karmann was already preparing to build BMW's coupés), and as a short-term measure Porsche reintroduced the 912 model, now powered by VW's fuel injected engine of 1,971 cc and developing 90 bhp. A total of 2,099 were built and shipped to the States in the 1976 model year, bridging the gap between the last 914 and the first 924.

By Porsche's standards the 924 was a pretty car, perhaps lacking in aggression, and this in itself gave it a wider appeal and made it popular with ladies too. The body was made entirely in galvanized steel, except for the fibreglass bumpers

Left *A transaxle system was adopted for the 924 model to gain an ideal weight distribution, using VW-Audi's four-speed manual or three-speed automatic transmissions. Torsion bar suspension was fitted at the rear.*

Right *The 924's front end stood up well to the compulsory 50 km/h crash test, though the dummy was left with a bad headache!*

which were on collapsible mountings. It had two seats in the back, suitable for children, and the backrest could be folded flat in order to double the luggage space (the platform was quite shallow, since the transmission was under the floor, but it was surprisingly capacious).

The radiator air intake was well-concealed underneath the front number plate, and could only be seen properly by someone in a kneeling position. The drag coefficient was just 0.36, an excellent figure for the day, and the overall gearing was particularly high to allow good cruising speeds to be combined with outstanding fuel economy figures. Initially VW-Audi's four-speed gearbox was installed, and for the 1977 model year the group's three-speed automatic transmission was offered.

Like the 911, the 924 carried a six-year warranty against rust holes, and it was introduced at the very reasonable price of DM23,450, the automatic version costing an extra DM1,500. Throughout the 924 model's life it was powered by a Bosch fuel-injected version of the Audi 2-litre, four-cylinder engine developing 125 bhp at 5,800 rpm, and 121.4 lb/ft of torque at 3,500 rpm. Unlike the Alfa Romeo Alfetta model, which had a fairly poor gearchange in its trans-axle system due to clutch inertia, the 924's clutch was at the front in a conventional position, and drive was taken to the rear by means of a torque tube, ¾ in (20 mm) in diameter but nearly 6 ft 6 in (2 m) in length. Running on four bearings, it proved smooth and completely trouble-free.

The suspension and brakes were very conventional, as many parts as possible being bought from VW. MacPherson struts were featured at the front, along with rack and pinion steering and solid brake discs, while at the rear the 924 featured fabricated semi-trailing arms, torsion bars kept the overall height to a minimum, and drum brakes were installed.

By laying the engine over at an angle of 40°, the bonnet line was kept low, but the view from the 911-type seats was less commanding, shall we say, than from a six-cylinder model; at first many owners ran with the headlamps raised, so that they could see the front corners! Anti-roll bars at the front and rear were optional, and in standard form the 924 came equipped with steel wheels, 14 inches (35.5 cm) in diameter, though alloy wheels were a popular option.

The 924 was what it set out to be, a grand touring car, capable of maintaining high average speeds in comfort and with economy. The handling was excellent, nicely balanced with a weight distribution of 52 per cent front, 48 per cent rear, the car would accelerate to 60 mph (96 km/h) in slightly less than 10 seconds (better than Porsche's own claim, though the *Motor* road test giving a figure of 8.2 seconds was probably optimistic), and the top speed was 125 mph (200 km/h). All this could be achieved with an average fuel consumption of 28-32 mpg (9-10 litres/100 km), a particularly good figure.

On the other hand the 924 was not, at first, quite as refined as it might have been. Road noise was fairly evident, cabin insulation was not as good as in a Lotus, for instance, and the engine developed a harshness at 4,800 rpm that was not particularly pleasant. Owners developed the habit of changing up to a higher gear at 4,500 rpm to use the torque curve, rather than the power curve, and still maintained high average speeds.

It should not have been surprising, therefore, that the 924 did not appeal straight away to Porsche enthusiasts, but the car was not intended for those who had ever owned a 911 anyway. Previous owners of 914 and 912 models were a target in marketing terms but more particularly, the 924 appealed to people who had never owned a Porsche before. . . and to those who had never even *considered* a Porsche.

Production of the 924 commenced, slowly at first, in February 1976 at the VW-Audi Neckarsulm factory. The body panels were stamped out, welded and formed there, the engines came from Salzgitter, suspension, brake and steering components from various VW sources, and only the seats came from the Porsche factory in Stuttgart. By July, the end of the model year, a total of 8,344 had been made and nearly all were sold in Germany.

The 1977 model year saw a complete transformation in Porsche's fortunes, led by the 924. A total of 23,180 four-cylinder cars, bearing the Porsche badge, were made at Neckarsulm and immediately the 924 became the most successful model ever made by the company; total exports to America topped 20,000 for the first time and a useful profit of DM17 million was seen on the balance sheet.

Minor modifications to the 924 included a roller-blind cover for the luggage, the standardization of a small centre console, in front of the gear lever, carrying an oil pressure gauge and a voltmeter, and the addition of hard rubber protecting strips along the sides. Then to celebrate the double World Championship racing successes of 1976, a special 'Martini' version was produced in January 1977.

Right *The 924 had ample seating for two adults, and space for two small children as well. The plastic fascia was unappealing, and instruments and controls came from VW's stock.*

Right *Introduced for the 1977 model year was a roller blind to cover the luggage; the rear seat backrest folded flat to allow more baggage space than in many saloons.*

Below *Less aggressive and more aesthetic than the 911, the 924 found no favour among Porsche die-hards but made many new friends for the marque.*

Above *To celebrate Porsche's double World Championship racing successes in 1976, a special 'Martini' version of the 924 was produced early in 1977.*

Below *Among several endurance trials to 'prove' the 924, Austrian Gerhard Plattner drove a car from Badwater, 280 feet below sea level at Salt Lake, to the 14,264 ft peak of Mount Evans. Temperatures ranged from 50°C at Badwater to −1° at the peak.*

Finished in white, with tasteful side-stripes in Martini's rainbow colours, the special 924 became a popular model. The alloy wheels were lacquered in white, the floor mats and boot carpet were scarlet, and the seats were piped with blue and red leather. Front and rear anti-roll bars were added as standard, with a detachable sunroof which was a popular option and a commemorative plaque, and Porsche was able to offer a model that still had a premium value ten years later.

With production running on target at 100 cars per day, the 924 was proving an unqualified success for Porsche, its dealer network, and for VW-Audi as well, the Neckarsulm plant now being a good profit-centre for its owners. For the 1978 model year (starting in September 1977, as is usual) the 924 underwent the most important change of its life when the rear suspension subframe was rubber mounted, substantially reducing the input of noise and vibration to the cabin. Fine tuning on the dampers ensured that the handling quality was not spoiled in the least, and Porsche's own five-speed manual gearbox became an option offering a closer match of ratios, fifth being the approximate equivalent of fourth in the Audi box. Not everyone liked the Porsche box, first being out and down to the left, and right-hand drive markets such as Britain deplored the quality of the shift as it entailed a difficult arm movement.

The 1978 model was distinguished by an oval rather than circular chromed exhaust tailpipe, and as options the factory offered uprated shock absorbers, electrically-operated window lifters and stove-enamelled black alloy wheels, the latter getting around the cleaning difficulties of the cheap looking aluminium-coloured spokes.

The British importers, headed by John Aldington, announced a one-make Porsche 924 Championship for 1978 in conjunction with the British Automobile Racing Club, and this is the first record of the four-cylinder model being used in competitions. In 1976 the Austrians Rudi Lins and Gerhard Plattner had undertaken a round-the-world drive in a 924 covering 13,864 miles (23,312 kilometres) in just 28 days, a very thorough test of the design, but a racing championship would bring the message home to the British and European markets.

Tests with the 924 showed it to be entirely suitable for racing, with fine handling and adequate power. Dunlop made some special slick tyres for the competitors, nearly all of whom were sponsored by dealers, the standard exhaust system was retained, and a limited amount of tuning was allowed—the standard power output of 98-101 bhp at the rear wheels was limited to 120 bhp on Porsche's rolling road at Reading, and this was attained without much more than blueprinting the engine and cleaning out the ports. As for the brakes, the drivers quickly learned how to pace them for 10 or 20 laps, and the 924 even competed successfully in the 750 Motor Club's 6-Hour relay races at Silverstone and Donington. More than 1,000 Porsches were sold in Britain for the first time, and more than half of those were 924s.

Within 26 months of production commencing, the 50,000th 924 was manufactured, but this proved to be the peak for this model. No changes were effected for the 1979 model year in which 20,632 924s were made, though 2,447 of the new 924 Turbo model should be added to this figure. Sales to America had numbered 13,696 in 1977, 10,483 in 1978 and 8,387 in 1979, a worrying trend exacerbated by the declining state of the dollar. The graph flattened out in 1980 and 1981 at just over 5,000 Porsche 924s, fortunately augmented in 1982 by slightly more than 5,000 944s, and in 1983 the 924 was withdrawn from the American market.

Two variations on the 924 engine were developed at Weissach and revealed in 1979, one type running on a methanol fuel mixture and the other with an experimental 'TOP' (Thermodyamically Optimum Porsche) cylinder head; both delivered 130 bhp, five more than the production unit. Fuel consumption was again a leading topic as prices soared for the second time in the decade, and Porsche was also experimenting with a 928 that would run on just four cylinders at urban speeds, and would stop the engine completely when stationary. All such experiments were discontinued in 1981 when the situation eased, but the TOP high-compression solution was certainly to benefit all production models later on.

The methanol experiment was part of a programme initiated by the German government, and the nation's industry built a total of 800 cars which would run on alternative fuels. Porsche's contribution was a fleet of ten 924s with compressions raised from 9.3:1 to 12.5:1, and able to run with 15 per cent of methanol added to normal petrol. The engine ran cooler and very clean in emissions, as well as being more economical. Plastic parts had to be replaced in the fuel system, though, as methanol is definitely detrimental, and the K-Jetronic injection system had to be adapted as well. The experimental 924 engine would run just as well on aethanol, which is produced biologically from beetroot, sugar cane or cereals.

So far as Porsche was concerned TOP was of more immediate interest, and involved a higher compression ratio (of between 11:1 and 13:1), improved combustion chamber shape, a leaner air/fuel mixture and different ignition settings. Detonation (knocking) was prevented by the high intensity 'swirl' shape of the combustion chamber, and all the lessons learned from the TOP exercise have subsequently been incorporated in production models.

Further improvements were carried out on the 924 in September 1979 (1980 model year) which completed its transformation to an appealing model. The Turbo had already been launched for those who sought extra performance, and the only change that would ever be carried out on the standard engine was the adoption of transistorized ignition, without affecting the power output. More importantly Audi's uprated five-speed gearbox became standard equipment, this having a much nicer quality than Porsche's ageing transmission and the first four gears in a conventional H-pattern, fifth being to the right and up, opposite reverse.

The brake servo was increased in diameter from 7 in to 9 in (178 mm to 229 mm), with a marked reduction in pedal effort, a remote-control mirror became standard on the driver's door (far better, with a plastic cowl, than the original metal-backed mirrors, which soon rusted), and an automatically-operated lamp was introduced to the luggage compartment. This model, the best so far, was distinguished by 'black look' door window surrounds and by a flap over the unattractive VW fuel filler cap.

The last important revision for the 2-litre 924, in 1983, included a spoiler around the rear window and the option of spoke-effect four-stud wheels.

One year later further specification changes were announced for the 924, including a seven-year corrosion warranty (the extent of galvanizing had been increased, now including the roof). The front anti-roll bar became standard equipment, and at the rear the suspension torsion bars were increased in stiffness as a means of reducing roll and thus improving the handling. More sound-proofing material was specified, direction lamps were seen on the sides of the front wings (as on the 911 models), twin air horns from the Turbo model were fitted, and a fog lamp incorporated at the rear. New options included full cloth trim for the seats, or special sport seats, and a cassette box centre armrest.

Another option for the 924, and standard on the special 'Le Mans' model, was a new style of spoke-effect alloy wheels, still with a 6J section but 15 in (38 cm) in diameter and carrying 205 section 60-series tyres. They were still a four-stud fixing, the Turbo having the 911's five-stud hubs, but they brought the 924 closer to the Turbo in appearance.

The Le Mans version, announced in June 1980 to commemorate the 924's debut at Le Mans, included a whole package of appealing features. It had the 15 in (38 cm) diameter wheels and 60-series tyres, the Turbo's polyurethane spoiler around the rear glass reducing the drag figure to 0.33, stiffer dampers and thicker anti-roll bars. The Turbo model's leather-covered, 14 in (36 cm) diameter steering wheel was standard in this package and the interior was uplifted with leather trim, the seats being black with white piping. If anyone is looking for a collectable 2-litre 924, this is the one! All the Le Mans models were distinguished by Alpine white paintwork with coloured side stripes.

In common with the full range the 924's roof was strengthened for the 1982 model year, the roof rack load being uprated from 75 lb to 165 lb (35 kg to 75 kg), and in 1983 the 2-litre underwent its last revision, the neat rear spoiler being standardized. Further additional sound-proofing was introduced, and the interior

Not a 924 Turbo as it seems, this 924 driven on the 1979 Monte Carlo Rally by Jürgen Barth and Roland Kussmaul. The turbo-charged engine was not homologated in time for the event.

trim improved to match that of the 944. The 911's well-padded, leather three-spoke steering wheel was standardized too, moving the 924 further away from the VW image. Synchromesh was introduced to reverse gear, and a four-speaker system was standardized for the radio.

In 1982 an electrically-tilting sunroof was introduced as an option, from the 944, and at long last an electric switch made it possible to release the tailgate glass from the driver's seat. New interior trims included a cloth with the Porsche name woven in. Then, for the tenth and final year of production the 924 owner benefited from heated windscreen washer nozzles and a graduated tint on the front glass.

It would be a pity if the 2-litre 924 was remembered by its early reputation, for by 1980 it had become a refined car and the improvements continued. The engine never became any smoother, but extra sound-proofing certainly helped, and although cheaper sports saloons such as the Golf GTi and the Ford XR3i could out-accelerate the 924, often to the owner's embarrassment, it was always the better car for all-day journeys at high averages.

924S takes over

It was neither desirable nor necessary to continue the 924 model for long, once the 944 was launched. . .not, at least, with the Audi-based 2-litre engine. A 924 equipped with the 2.5-litre counterbalanced engine was always 'do-able', to quote

The 2-litre Porsche 924 (above) was replaced by the 2.5-litre 924S in 1985. The important difference was in the engine bay, but to distinguish the newcomer Porsche produced some special alloy wheels reminiscent of those of the eight-cylinder 928 model.

Peter Schutz's phrase, but would show no great cost savings. In its twilight years the 924 had been a particular favourite in Britain, where combined four-cylinder model sales reached 2,362 in 1983, and in Italy where a government tax of 18 per cent on cars up to 2-litres jumped to 38 per cent on cars above that arbitrary capacity level. A 2-litre version of the counterbalanced engine was considered too, but rejected on the grounds that a smaller bore would be outside Porsche's block-building system, and that it could be made no less expensively.

Certain markets, though, still needed an entry-level Porsche, so it was decided to install the counterbalanced engine into the 924 shape, a step that necessarily involved adopting the 944's uprated suspension system, disc brake system, five-stud wheel fixings, and steering. Alloy wheels of 6J section, carrying 195 section tyres, would be the widest available to fit the narrower arches, and it was then realized that with a smaller frontal cross-section than a 944, the 924S might actually be quicker! Back to the drawing board, and the 944's compression ratio of 10.6:1, aiding a power output of 163 bhp, was reduced to 9.7:1 ostensibly to enable it to run on 91 octane fuel; this was correct, but the power output was reduced to 150 bhp, the maximum speed of 133 mph (213 km/h) being a little short of the 944's 137 mph (219 km/h). Just the same, those in the know could detect no difference between a good 924S and an average 944.

Rather more to the point, Porsche was able to offer the 924S with catalytic equipment with the 150 bhp figure maintained, the performance being identical. The 944, on the other hand, lost 8 bhp to a total of 155 bhp when fitted with emission equipment. For 1988, however, the 924S and the 944 were given a common 160 bhp 8-valve engine with no loss of power in emission-controlled form.

Still retaining the familiar 924 interior, the 2.5-litre S version now had yellow figures upon black dials, and other improvements introduced during the 1980s had certainly made it a desirable package, introduced in the autumn of 1985 for the 1986 model year. In Britain, though, the pound was going through one of its periodic slumps against the strong Deutschmark, and Porsche prices were raised by an average of 30 per cent in the 1986 calendar year, that of the 924S rising to £18,464—a far cry from the sub-£15,000 price tag on the model when it was introduced.

_____924 Turbo—new-found power_____

Given that real Porsche fans found it hard to welcome the 924 to their hearts, a way was needed to give it more appeal. There was only one way the Weissach engineers knew how, and that was to give the 1,984 cc engine more power, by turbo-charging. The bottom end of the engine was capable of withstanding considerably more power without major modifications, the main one being to increase oil flow around the bearings, and development concentrated on the cylinder head, which was entirely new.

The shape of the combustion chamber was changed, the spark plugs being moved to the induction area, and the valves were made of materials with higher heat resistance, those on the exhaust side being ⅛ in (3 mm) greater in diameter.

Above *For the 1988 model year the 924S had the same 160 bhp power unit as the 944.*

Below and right *With the help of a KKK turbocharger and a new cylinder head Porsche increased the 924's power to 170 bhp, substantially improving the performance. Better brakes, suspension and transmission formed parts of the package.*

A KKK turbo-charger was installed, finding a home underneath the exhaust pipe manifold, and became usefully effective at 2,800 rpm, with a wastegate valve pressure of 0.7 bar. Although the compression ratio was reduced to 7.5:1 there was a substantial rise in power, to 170 bhp at 5,500 rpm, while torque was increased even more notably by 50 per cent to 181 lb/ft at 3,500 rpm.

There were numerous other changes. The front and rear suspensions were reworked, ventilated disc brakes were fitted at front and rear, and the 911's five-stud wheel fixings allowed the fitment of new pattern 6J × 15 in (38 cm) or 6J × 16 in (40.5 cm) wheels. The torque tube carrying drive to the trans-axle was thickened in diamter, from ¾ in to 1 in (20 mm to 25 mm) and the driveshafts were strengthened too. The clutch was increased to 8¾ in (225 mm) in diameter, like the 911's, with hydraulic control, and in the Porsche five-speed gearbox the first and second ratios were lowered.

An oil cooler was incorporated at the front, air being ducted to this and to the brakes from slots above and below the bumper line, and a NACA duct in the bonnet reduced the temperature when the car was stationary. There were some very attractive dual colour schemes and, with a polyurethane spoiler around the rear window reducing the drag figure slightly to 0.35, the 924 Turbo was a most attractive model visually.

All the engines were built at Zuffenhausen, rather than Salzgitter, and each was bench-tested before installation at Neckarsulm. In this, and other ways, the 924 Turbo came much closer to the standards expected of Porsche and road tests confirmed that the model would have a bright future. The factory's performance figures were regularly bettered, the official ones including a time of 7.8 seconds from standstill to 62 mph (100 km/h), 28 seconds for the standing kilometre (three seconds quicker than a 924), and a top speed of 140 mph (225 km/h).

The fuel consumption need have been no higher than that of a 924, driven with restraint, since the steady speed figures were comparable, but owners tended to use the extra performance wherever possible and the average figures tended to be in the 23 to 28 mpg (10-12 litres/100 km) range. The handling was a little better than the 924's although wider wheels could not be fitted inside the standard arches, and braking was infinitely better; the 928's floating calipers on ventilated discs made a world of difference, and, although the Turbo model was 64 lb (29 kg) heavier at the front it did not become an understeering car, as careful suspension tuning maintained the correct feel through the smaller-diameter, four-spoke steering wheel.

If there was any criticism to be levelled at the 924 Turbo it concerned the rather sudden arrival of power at 3,000 rpm, a characteristic of the turbo-charger, all too reminiscent of the early model 911 Turbo. It was, of course, easier to control 170 bhp than 260 bhp, and it was just something the owners learned to live with.

Changes for the 1980 model year were minor, in line with the 924's and including a flap over the fuel filler cap, but for the 1981 model year the 924 Turbo was usefully refined. The adoption of digital ignition (DZV, standing for Digitalelektronische Zündzeitpunkt Verstellung) previewed in the Carrera GT

Above *In performance the 944 Turbo ran closest to the 911 Carrera, though its characteristics are entirely different.*

Below *In 1979 Porsche offered high performance in three packages: the 924 Turbo, the 911 Turbo and the 928S.*

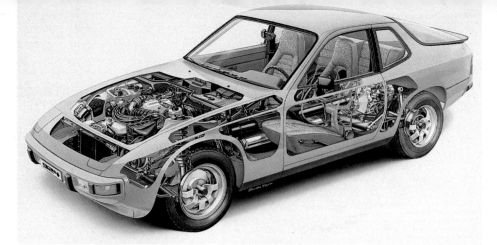

Above *Porsche's 924, styled at Weissach and introduced in 1975, was needed to widen the company's model range. Its lines were timeless, and in particular the radiator ducting — below the front number plate — offered a neat solution. This was, after all, the first Porsche to have water cooling, and there was no need to advertise the fact!*

Below *The Porsche 944S, with four valves per cylinder, was introduced as a stepping-stone between the 163 bhp, 8-valve 944 model and the 220 bhp 944 Turbo. It would also offer better performance than the 944 with catalytic equipment in place, a compelling sales advantage in many work markets.*

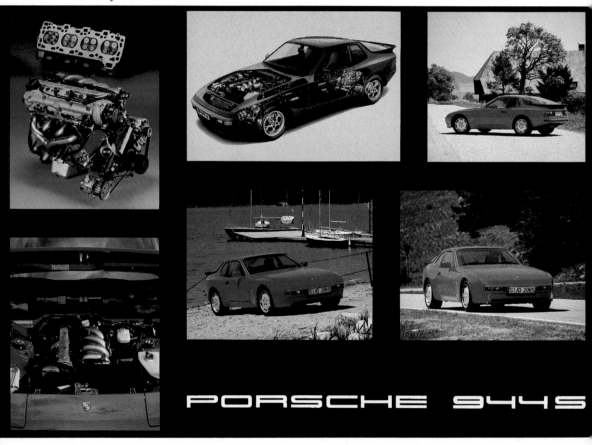

PORSCHE 944S

model enabled Porsche to raise the compression ratio to 8.5:1, a remarkably high figure for a turbo-charged engine (especially one that did not have an inter-cooler). Sensors monitoring engine speeds, boost pressure, compressed air temperature and detonation enabled the ignition settings to be programmed constantly, and the driving characteristic was much improved with the adoption of a smaller, faster-reacting KKK turbo-charger. Power increased from 170 to 177 bhp, while a very modest increase in torque, to 184.5 lb/ft at the same engine speed, 3,500 rpm, tended to disguise the real improvement in driveability. The top speed went up to 143 mph (230 km/h), the 0-60 mph time came down to 7.5 seconds, yet the average fuel consumption figure was improved by 13 per cent.

Worldwide sales of the 924 Turbo did not exceed 12,000 in the four years of the car's life, which is a pity because it was a well-liked model, exceedingly quick in Porsche tradition yet quiet in operation, and economical. The 924 Carrera GT made in limited numbers diverted attention from the 924 Turbo, and when the new 944 model reached production stage in the autumn of 1981 the Zuffenhausen engine department needed to work flat-out to produce Porsche's very own four-cylinder power unit. Except for a handful of 924 Turbos destined for the Italian market, the model was discontinued in the summer of 1982.

Carrera GT

The 924's acceptability was firmly established by the Turbo model in 1978, and at the Frankfurt Show in September 1979 the 924 Carrera GT was unveiled. Even in black there was nothing understated about the car, which had Carrera signwriting in scarlet script on one massively-flared front wheel arch. The front wings were made of the 928's bouncy polyurethane material, as were the tack-on rear arch extensions (designer Lapine invited me to criticize the appearance, and expected the response that the car looked aggressive enough, but rather messy). It was, though we did not know it, a preview of the 944 and Turbo models which would come later, with a completely finished appearance.

The 2-litre engine, still based on the 924 and Turbo block, had the benefit of an air-to-air intercooler which made high boost pressures safer to achieve, and the compression ratio was increased to 8.5:1, helped by a new digital ignition system. The power rose to a heady 210 bhp, torque to 202.5 lb/ft at 3,500 rpm, and the Carrera's maximum speed was a genuine 150 mph (240 km/h), with 60 mph being reached in under seven seconds.

Extremely high performance was guaranteed although, like the 924 Turbo and more so, the rather abrupt arrival of 210 bhp could be quite exciting in rainy weather. The NACA duct on the bonnet was replaced by an air scoop, the four turbo slots in the nose panel were retained, and a new air dam (also in polyurethane) improved the general appearance of the Carrera and lowered the drag figure to 0.34.

Just 400 examples of the Carrera GT were made, 200 being sold in Germany, 75 in Britain and the remaining 125 in other European markets, and they were

The four-cylinder range was taken further up the performance scale with the unveiling of the Carrera GT in 1979. Widened wheel arches, made of polyurethane, allowed the fitment of much wider wheels (these from the 928S), though the bonnet-mounted air intake was changed before the model's first public showing in September.

available in any colour you liked so long as it was black, white or red! They were the meanest-looking 924s ever made, without doubt, lowered on their Bilstein strut suspensions and equipped with 911 Turbo-type wheels, of 15 in (38 cm) 205 section or, optionally, with 16 in (40.5 cm) wheels with 205/55 Pirelli P7 tyres at the front and 225/50 section tyres at the rear.

The 400 cars were easily sold in the first half of 1980, those allocated to the British market being snapped up despite a pricey tag of £19,210, about the same as a 911 SC, and were soon commanding premium prices. The German price was DM60,000 and the German dealers had no difficulty in selling their 200 examples.

924s and 944s in competitions

When Rudi Lins and Gerhard Plattner completed their marathon runs in the 924 and then the 924 Turbo, they were competing against the elements and putting the finishing touches to the pre-production endurance trials undertaken by the

Just 400 924 Carrera GT models were made, and there was a healthy demand for this limited supply. With intercoolers, the 2-litre engines developed 210 bhp. This version, built for homologation, was a forerunner of the 220 bhp 944 Turbo.

development teams. The 924 model had its circuit baptism in 1978 when Porsche Cars Great Britain Ltd sponsored an eight-race one-make series, the cars virtually in standard trim and running with normal silencing equipment. No mechanical problems were experienced during the season, and the series was well won by Tony Dron, driving for Gordon Ramsay Limited, ahead of Andy Rouse (Heddell and Deeks Motors). The following year the 924 Championship specification cars were able to establish new British 2,000 kilometre and 24-hour speed and endurance records on the Snetterton race circuit at 76 mph (122 km/h), the only breakdown of any sort being a broken throttle cable on the AFN Ltd entry (Tony Dron/Andy Rouse/Win Percy) which established the 24-hour record.

In January 1979 Porsche's Jürgen Barth, accompanied by Roland Kussmaul, drove a 924 (with 924 Turbo suspension) in the Monte Carlo Rally, and later in the year undertook the arduous Australian Repco Rally to finish eighth overall and win the 2-litre class.

For the American SCCA racing series, Porsche built a series of 16 special 924s, also with Turbo-type uprated suspension and all-disc braking. The 924 SCCA, as it was officially called, continued to use the normally-aspirated Audi based engine but with the bore increased slightly to take the capacity to 2,039 cc. Bosch/Kugelfischer mechanical fuel injection replaced the usual K-Jetronic, the compression was raised to 11.5:1 and the power rose to 180 bhp at 7,000 rpm, making this quite a respectable machine for the American amateur drivers. Dry sump lubrication was installed, and the SCCA version was easily the quickest of all normally-aspirated 924s, performance helped by some drastic weight-reductions which brought the car down to 2,140 lb (970 kg).

The announcement of the turbo-charged Carrera GT in September 1979 spelled the end of development for normally-aspirated engines, of course, and at the beginning of 1980 it was announced that the Porsche factory would compete at Le Mans with the evolutionary 924 GTR. This was to the 924 Turbo base model what the 935 had been to the 911 Turbo, retaining only the bare monocoque and installing a host of advanced features. Fully coil-sprung suspension replaced torsion bars at the rear (the springs were made of titanium), hubs were from the 935, and the massive disc brake system was similar to that on the old 917, though with the 936's calipers.

A 2-litre capacity was retained for the engine, still using Audi's bore and stroke, but extensive work at the top end raised the power output to 320 bhp at 7,000 rpm, giving the car a maximum speed of around 176 mph (282 km/h). The transmission was well reinforced, the differential for instance being locked solid, in Porsche's customary manner. The weight was reduced to 2,046 lb (930 kg) and the GTR was clad extensively with lightweight materials that gave it quite a different, wider look.

Three 924 Carrera GTRs were to race at Le Mans instead of the 936s, a contro-versial decision made by Professor Fuhrmann, and it was intended that they would be driven by factory mechanics and qualified amateur drivers, in order to avoid the impression that the factory was actually trying to win the race with a production car! If I may take a mite of credit, I suggested instead that they should be allocated to 'national' teams, German, British and American perhaps, and this is what actually happened. It was then decided that since they were works cars, some professional drivers should after all be involved, and Derek Bell was persuaded to give up an attractive drive in a privately-owned 935 to lead the British entry, with Tony Dron and Andy Rouse.

At Le Mans, Peter Gregg was concussed in a nasty road accident before he had even driven the 'American' entry, so Derek Bell moved across to partner Al Holbert; Dron and Rouse drove the 'British' entry, Jürgen Barth and Manfred Schurti the 'German' entry. Each car was beautifully liveried by the British stylist employee Arnold Ostle, with national flags on the bonnets and rear wings.

Trials at the Ricard circuit had gone well, but a transmission breakage stopped the GTR after 28 hours, and after repairs the car ran another four hours before burning an exhaust valve. With hindsight, everyone wondered how it had lasted that long.

As expected, the three 924 Carrera GTRs were right on the borderline in qualifying for the 24-Hour race, but rain in the first hour of the race allowed Bell to show all his expertise, lapping the less-experienced Rouse and pulling away half a lap from Barth. Through the night the three cars ran beautifully, placed eighth, ninth and tenth on Sunday morning, but then two of them, the British and American entries, burned exhaust valves and slowed badly. The fuel mixture was richened on Barth's car and he finished a praiseworthy sixth overall, better than Porsche had dared hope for, but the other two were very lame as they finished twelfth and thirteenth.

The GT Rally was specially built for World Champion Walter Röhrl to campaign in 1981, when his contract with Mercedes fell through. His events were confined to the German Championship.

Capitalizing on this experience, Porsche then laid down a series of competitions models which were built in the first half of 1981, but it proved difficult to sell them. A total of 59 GTS versions were built, virtually Carrera GT in specification but with 245 bhp or 275 bhp available from the turbo-charged 2-litre engine. All were painted red, and the asking price was DM110,000.

The GTS, though stripped out and lacking creature comfort, still weighed 2,466 lb (1,121 kg), but the Group 4 competitions homologated car was taken a further stage in evolution with a series of 19 GTR production cars, each weighing 2,079 lb (945 kg) (titanium, where it had been used, was replaced by heavier though less-expensive materials) and costing DM145,000. The 937, the type number allocated to the racing version, had a nominal power rating of 280 bhp, while for a grand outlay of DM180,000 a full 'Le Mans' version could be bought with a maximum of 375 bhp.

The adoption of a new Kugelfischer injection pump was one of a few modifications, but against better opposition—which included factory 936s—the three cars seen at Le Mans did not fare well. Richard Lloyd's had engine problems throughout practice and failed to qualify, the Almeras brothers went out with a broken gearbox after two hours, and only Manfred Schurti/Andy Rouse had anything like a decent run to eleventh place overall, while covering one lap fewer than Barth/Schurti had the year before, when placed sixth. They were inevitably overshadowed by the winning 936 driven by Ickx and Bell, and by another '924 GTP' which should, had the model been announced, have been called the '944 GTP'.

The production-based 924 engine had performed with some distinction, but the abiding recollection is the battle with failing exhaust valves, difficulties in qualifying and so on. . . and the customers did not exactly queue up to buy them, even though the popular German rally driver, Walter Rohrl, drove a 924

Above left *From the 924 Carrera GT evolved the GTR (nearest camera), the GTS and the GT Rally. Engine power ranged from 245 to 375 bhp, but these versions were no-one's favourites.*

Above *The entire production of 924 Carera GTS models totalled 59 cars, all painted red and priced at DM110,000. Before despatch they are lined up for FIA homologation inspection, with engines rated at 245 or 275 bhp.*

Middle right and right *The 'production' 924 Carera GTR models were offered with a maximum of 375 bhp and cost DM180,000. Nineteen were made, but cylinder head weakness limited their appeal.*

Left *Porsche's main assault at Le Mans in 1980 was limited to a trio of 924 Carrera GTR models, tastefully presented with national flags of Germany, Britain and America. Two burned exhaust valves but all three finished, the Barth/Schurti entry in sixth place overall.*

Right *Raced as a '924 GT Prototype', Porsche's four-cylinder entry at Le Mans in 1981 was in fact a prototype of the 944 Turbo. It was and may remain unique in having a turbo-charger and a 16-valve cylinder head, to develop 420 bhp.*

GTR to some good placings in the 1981 German Rally Championship. So how is the 924 GTR now regarded at Weissach?

With the passage of time Professor Bott can afford to be honest. 'I like Black Forest cake. It has rich ingredients, chocolate, cream and cherries, you know. But if I give you some sand and a bucket of water, you cannot make a Black Forest cake that I would enjoy. It was like that with the 924. We did the best with the engine we had, but all the time we were thinking of the 944, which raced in 1981. . .'

The debut of the 924 GTP at Le Mans in 1981, only days before the 944 road car was announced, was auspicious. All the basic development work of the body, suspension and transmission had been carried out the previous year, so all that remained to be done was to fit the prototype 2.5-litre four-cylinder engine, install thicker brake discs to cope with the higher speeds, and go testing at the Ricard circuit. The car nominally weighed 2,090 lb (950 kg), though in Le Mans trim it was rather heavier at 2,196 lb (998 kg).

There was, naturally, a marked reluctance to raise the bonnet on the 924 GTP, for it concealed the Porsche engine, in effect half a 928, with a 4 in (100 mm) bore and 3¼ in (78.9 mm) stroke. Such an engine would be difficult to balance were it not for the twin, counter-rotating 'balancer shifts' driven by cogged belts, which really did make it as silky as a good six-cylinder, or even a V8. The cylinder head was a 16-valve design, which is noteworthy because a 16-valve turbo is not, even now, envisaged for the production line. A single KKK turbo-

Above *Despite experiencing severe head sealing problems during trials, the 2.5-litre turbo-charged '924 GT Prototype' ran beautifully to seventh place overall at Le Mans in the hands of Barth and Röhrl.*

Below *Prior to the debut of the 944 Turbo model, a prototype handsomely won the Nelson Ledges 24-hour production sports car race in America in 1984. It was driven by Jim Busby/Rick Knoop/Freddy Baker and, remarkably, it was fitted with catalytic equipment.*

charger boosted at 1.1 bar (15.5 lb), with an intercooler to lower the temperature of the compressed air, and the engine was unique in racing in having the full Bosch engine management system, a prototype of Motronic, with computer control for fuel flow, injection, ignition, boost pressure and knock control (and, like the 924 Carrera GTPs of the year before, it also ran with a Bosch/Porsche tyre pressure sensing device, later to be featured on the 959 model).

Early tests with the 944 prototype, at the Ricard circuit, had been conducted with a boost pressure of 1.3 bar (18.3 lb), at which the engine developed 450 bhp, but this was too much for the cylinder head, and sealing problems on the 'open deck' design were worrying. An engine had been tested on a bench at Weissach without the counterbalance shafts, as these absorbed five horsepower, but vibration was so severe that they were replaced. As raced, the 2,479 cc engine developed 420 bhp at 5,800 rpm, with 1.1 bar (15.5 lb) boost pressure.

The 944 prototype had a marvellously trouble-free run at Le Mans in the hands of Walter Rohrl and Jürgen Barth, stopping for fuel only 21 times on its way to seventh place overall. It also earned a special trophy for spending the least time of any in the pits, 56 minutes altogether, and since the fuel flow was restricted to 50 litres per minute at refuelling, it appears that no time could have been cut from the total.

The track debut of the 944 was perfect for Porsche, since the race had been won by their 936, and the stage was set for the new model's announcement. The '924 GTP', if we must call it that, raced only once more, but a successor was built . . . in America.

Straight after its run at Le Mans, the racing 944 turbo prototype was repainted and taken to the Norisring for the 'Supercup' race, to be driven by German rally champion Walter Röhrl.

In October 1985 Al Holbert, director of Porsche Motorsport North America in Warrington, Pennsylvania, announced that a series of eight 944 GTR racing cars would be built for customers in the IMSA and SCCA series, each priced at $100,000. These had full spaceframe chassis owing no allegiance to the factory, and type 962 brakes, though visually they strongly resembled the 924 GTP. The weight, though, was down to 1,993 lb (906 kg) including ballast to meet a class limit.

Four years of progress allowed PCNA to announce the racing engine with 525 bhp, aided by a 1.6 bar (22.5 lb) boost pressure, even though a normal two-valve per cylinder head was used. Despite the extremely light weight and abundance of power, the 944 GTR's maximum speed was quoted at 175 mph (280 km/h), about the same as for the 320 bhp 924 GTR raced by Holbert himself in 1980; it was surely under-estimated.

944: Porsche's jewel

A large capacity four-cylinder engine was seemingly the least-likely option open to Porsche for a new model, one which would make use of the 924's basic bodyshell. There was no room for a V8, admittedly, and nor should the car try to compete with the 928, but a V6 was the least that customers might expect. A V6 version of the V8, effectively with two cylinders lopped off and a capacity of 3.5-litres, was tested but found to be basically imbalanced, and fuel thirsty. Then the PRV (Peugeot-Renault-Volvo) V6 was installed in a 924, but no-one really liked it.

The four-cylinder project began in 1977, only two years into the 924's life, when it became clear that the best economical solution would be to make use of the 928's technology. One bank of the 4,474 cc engine would produce a nice, light 2.2-litre slant-four, with capability of being taken out to 2.5-litres. Such an engine, however, must needs be inherently well-balanced (vibration was a continuing source of criticism of the Audi engine, at higher speeds), and a Weissach brainstorming session came up with the answer: go back to Dr Frederick Lanchester's age-old, patent-elapsed balancer shaft invention.

The team went to work, testing prototype units with different shafts at different heights, and was satisfied eventually with a twin balancer shaft system, with vertically-arranged shafts counter rotating and driven by the same cogged belt as the single overhead camshaft. In Japan, the Mitsubishi company made much of the fact that it had already incorporated the balancer shaft system in its engine range, but this was shrugged off by Porsche who merely sought an ideal solution, wherever it came from.

Although the bore dimension of 4 in (100 mm) was larger than that of the 4.5-litre 928 model 3¾ in (95 mm) and wouldn't match up exactly until the 5-litre 928S-4 was introduced, the 3⅛ in (78.9 mm) stroke was identical and enabled Porsche to use the same connecting rods as well as similar cylinder heads, camshafts, valves and hydraulic buckets and various other useful items.

PCNA Competitions director Al Holbert had eight special Porsche 944 Turbos made in 1986, with full spaceframe chassis and down to 906 kg. Though with 8-valve cylinder heads, the 944 GTR model was said to develop 525 bhp.

Above *The 944 model, announced in June 1981, was largely based upon the 924 but with the 2.5-litre engine, improved suspension, brakes and transmission, and with wider wheel arches.*

Below *The 944's engine was derived from that of the 928, though with important differences. In order to 'drown' the vibrations of a 2.5-litre four-cylinder twin, counter-rotating balancer shafts were installed, so successfully that the perception was of a six or eight-cylinder unit.*

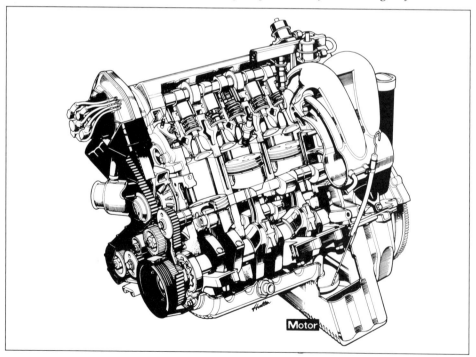

The polyurethane air dam on the 944 model, in conjunction with the nicely flared body arches, improved the four-cylinder model's appearance handsomely.

The crankcase needed to be redesigned and the block needed to accommodate the balance shafts, which ran at twice crankshaft speed. Like the 928 it is a linerless 'open deck' design in Renolds aluminium, produced on the same machinery as makes the V8, and the bores were Nikasil treated to reduce friction.

The cylinder head was particularly interesting since the combustion chambers incorporated, exactly, the TOP (Thermodynamically Optimum Porsche) technique, with wedge-shaped chambers, parallel valves and a central spark plug position. The compression ratio was high, at 10.6:1, and the designers felt that they had achieved optimum thermodynamic efficiency; fuel consumption figures certainly bore out this view.

The Bosch L-Jetronic injection system was combined, for the first time, with digital ignition, the Motronic system, with micro-chip control of 256 functions covering the entire ignition 'map' and taking into account ambient temperature, engine temperature, load, knock, maximum engine speed (reducing the fuel flow above 6,500 rpm), and with a fuel cutout when slowing down.

The power output, 163 bhp at 5,800 rpm, was no more or less than anyone would have expected at 65 bhp/litre, but the torque curve was prodigious. The curve, though nearly flat, allowed at least 144 lb/ft (20 mkg) between 2,500 and 5,500 rpm, peaking at 151.2 lb/ft (20.9 mkg) at 3,000 rpm. Allied with the now excellent, reinforced Audi five-speed transmission the 944 was immediately regarded as a highly flexible model, easy to drive in any gear, and superbly quiet and well balanced; totally refined, in other words.

Porsche claimed only that the counterbalanced four-cylinder engine was comparable with a 'six', but it would even bear comparison with an average V8.

Insulating the engine from the occupants was a new mounting system, a pair of hollow cast, light alloy engine supports containing hydraulic rams, rather like a conventional shock absorber. The steering used more rubber bushes than usual in a Porsche without feeling at all woolly, and it was only in the suspension department that the 944 was capable of disappointment, with more road noise and rumble coming through than a discerning owner would like.

The 944's body was subtly widened in the way the Carrera GT had suggested, the front wings flared out and the rear side panels given a muscular bulge as well. The 944 could now easily accommodate larger wheels, 7J × 15 being standard with 185/70 VR tyres, and 16 in (40.5 cm) 7J forged wheels, Turbo pattern, being optional with 205/55 section tyres. Altogether the body was 2 in (5 cm) wider than that of the 924, though with a disproportionally more 'macho' and aggressive appearance. The front of the 944 was restyled with a polyurethane apron spoiler, with a full-width cooling slot underneath the radiator duct. The drag figure was the same as the 924 Turbo's, at 0.35.

Ventilated disc brakes, 11.23 in (28.25 cm) diameter at the front and 11.37 in (28.9 cm) diameter at the rear, were fitted with 928 type floating calipers.

Independent test figures, as usual, bettered the factory's claims, especially in acceleration. The standstill to 100 km/h figure, for instance, was said to be 8.4 seconds, but *Autocar* achieved a typical 7.4 seconds for the slightly shorter sprint to 60 mph, while confirming the top speed at 137 mph (219 km/h). The standing start kilometre occupied 29 seconds according to Porsche, and 28.7 seconds according to *Autocar*, the magazine also recording an average fuel consumption of 26.2 mpg (9.3 litres/100 km), including performance testing, with a worst tank figure of 24.9 mpg (9.3 litres/100 km). The tank had a 14.5 gallon (66 litre) capacity.

The 944's astonishing smoothness and flexibility was a key feature of the reviews, criticisms concentrating on the harsh-sounding ride and on the fact that the instruments, in particular, were still VW origined, though now with yellow figures on black dials. The steering wheel, from the 924 Turbo, was smaller in diameter than that of the 924, but still offered a tight fit for the driver's thighs. A completely new water flap valve heating and ventilation system was introduced for the 944, air conditioning being an optional extra, with better volume and control. The only feature marring the system was its inability to deliver cold air through the fascia vents while pumping warm air to the footwells.

In essence the 944 had something that the 924 did not, namely a 'proper Porsche' engine, the key to all the company's present and future thinking. It received a rapturous welcome in all markets, especially in America where, with 150 bhp in catalytic form, it excelled over the 924 that was about to be withdrawn. It was available, too, with Audi's three-speed automatic transmission, barely a second slower in acceleration to 60 mph (96 km/h), and respectable at last.

At Neckarsulm the Porsche line was itself practically turbo-charged in 1981, the output rising from 72 to 130 cars per day of which approximately 100 were

944 models, the remainder 924s and a very few 924 Turbos. Nearly all these engines, of course, were built at Zuffenhausen and each one was bench-tested, bringing about a rapid extension in facilities. In the 1983 model year, ending August, no fewer than 23,200 944s were built, already surpassing the 924's record peak, and the company was well on the road to prosperity.

Detail changes were introduced year by year, a four-speaker sound system coming with improved interior trim in 1982, and a full seven-year anti-corrosion warranty was offered. In 1983 power-assisted steering was offered as an option, a speed-related system derived from the 928S, along with an electric release for the rear hatch and electric tilting for the sunroof.

More significant improvements came by stages in 1985, several features having been delayed by the metalworkers' strike a few months before. Principally, the 944 and the newly-announced 944 Turbo had a completely new fascia design (seen for the first time in February, at the Stockholm motor show), curved away from the occupants and more reminiscent of the 928's design. The instruments were of a new design, the steering wheel was height-adjustable, and air flow through the fascia vents was increased by 35 per cent.

To ease production the 944 benefited from a good many of the new Turbo features, including a greater sump capacity and a larger pump, increasing oil flow by 10 per cent; the battery was moved from the front to the boot, and the fuel tank capacity was increased by 20 per cent to 17.6 gallons (80 litres). The front and rear suspensions were made stronger, in cast aluminium rather than forged steel, the fuse box and relays were moved from the passenger's footwell to the engine compartment, the starter motor became stronger and quieter, the alternator capacity was increased to 115 amps, and in order to reduce road noise the trans-axle mounting system was improved.

There were more features, too. The windscreen was now bonded in with a flush fit, and incorporated the radio antenna; as an option, the safer Sekuriflex windscreen became available, and for Britain, Australia, Japan and other right-hand drive markets, the wipers now parked on the left. The front seats were improved in design and mounted 1¼ in (30 mm) lower, with electric adjustment available as an option, while in the automatic version the gear selected was shown in a window in the tachometer dial.

The Frankfurt Show in 1985 produced a whole crop of 944 convertibles among the specialists, but none was as nice as the convertible that appeared on Porsche's own stand. The soft-top, an attractive design, was fully retractable and a new rear deck, incorporating a lockable luggage compartment, blended perfectly with the normal styling.

The 944 'study' was fitted with a 185 bhp 16-valve engine, still 2.5-litres, almost a year ahead of the 944S model. It also had an air bag safety system which would suit the American market, and a new generation ABS brake system which would call for revised suspension settings, with negative roll radius geometry.

While the 911 'study' of 1981 came only six months before the announcement of the 911 Cabriolet, there was no intention to rush the 944 Cabriolet into production. Anyone expecting it in 1986 or 1987 was disappointed, as the likely date for announcement was changed to March 1988, at the Geneva Show.

Absolute power

It was not difficult to foretell the arrival of a turbo-charged version of the 944. It had been raced at Le Mans in 1981, engineers had disclosed it in interviews and for two years Peter Schutz had spoken freely about the pleasures of driving it. The 944 Turbo was announced in February 1985, with production due to commence in July, at which time over 70,000 standard 944s had been made and sold.

The absolute power figure of 220 bhp was impressive enough, but it was also the original 'first class' model which would develop the same power, and

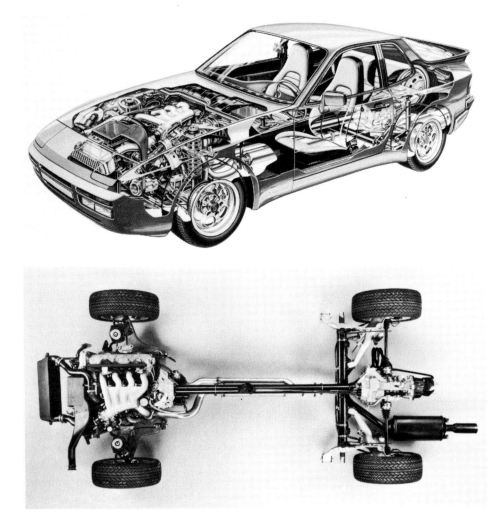

Right *A considerable amount of work went into the development of the 944 Turbo engine, not least in locating the turbo-charger on the 'cool' side of the engine, involving complicated exhaust plumbing.*

Left *The 944 Turbo was faithful to the original trans-axle concept, but in power and performance it was moving ever upwards. With an intercooler, the four-cylinder 2.5-litre turbo engine developed 220 bhp, and the car would exceed 150 mph.*

achieve exactly the same performance, with catalytic equipment, as project manager Jochen Freund announced at the unveiling in southern France. The powerful engine would run on leaded fuel, but was designed primarily to run on lead-free petrol down to 95 octane.

In terms of power and performance the 944 Turbo came very close to the 3.2 litre 911 Carrera (as it did on price), and exceeded the power of the much more aggressive 924 Carrera GT. Far from being a neck-jerking, all-or-nothing engine, the new one retained the 944's expansive torque curve and the arrival of boost from the turbo-charger was so silky that it seemed more like a lusty V8 engine being opened up under the bonnet.

The KKK-type K26 turbo-charger was a new design, with a water jacket lowering its operating temperature, and it was fitted on the cooler induction side of the engine with a crossover pipe from the exhaust passing behind the engine block; among several advantages were a 90° drop in temperature and a shorter passage to the induction manifold, virtually eliminating throttle lag. A new type of boost pressure regulator was designed to replace the traditional flap valve, reducing exhaust back-pressure and improving economy.

Unusually a water-cooled turbo heat-exchanger was introduced for the 944 Turbo, more efficient than the usual air-air intercooler. The engine block was reinforced in places to cope with the extra power, with thicker cylinder walls for instance, and the compression ratio was 8:1. An interesting detail was the use of ceramic liners in the exhaust ports of the cylinder head. Forged pistons were used instead of cast material and the crowns featured oval recesses, in the interest of combustion efficiency, instead of being flat-topped.

Improvements went right through the car. The five-speed gearbox, still Audi sourced, was considerably strengthened with special materials, the crownwheel was uprated and the ratios brought closer. The brake discs were now slowed by

a new design of calliper, made of aluminium (for better heat dissipation) with four piston plungers for each wheel, and the new polyurethane front spoiler was designed to duct air to the front callipers.

Aluminium forgings replaced steel for the front wishbones and rear semi-trailing arms—these were also transferred to the 944—and the gas strut shock absorbers were uprated, along with thicker anti-roll bars.

The new front air dam was complemented by a tray device at the back, under the bumper, designed to improve the under-body ducting and increase resistance to crosswinds. Together with the bonded, flush-fit windscreen the drag figure was reduced to 0.33, an extremely good figure for a car free of lift, while the Cx figure (Cd × frontal area) was a class-leading 0.624.

Very quick and very quiet was the verdict on the 944 Turbo. At low engine speeds, around 2,000 rpm, it pulled at least as well as the normally-aspirated 944, and the torque curve was virtually flat from 2,500 rpm to 5,500 rpm (peaking at 243 lb/ft (33.8 mkg) at 3,500 rpm) to ensure an even spread of response to the throttle.

With merely 35 lb (16 kg) added to the weight of the four-cylinder engine, power-assisted steering became a standard feature, but its unobtrusive weight and sporting nature complemented the car's characteristics on mountain roads. It did not really matter what gear the Turbo was in, it surged up the hills as though the road was flat, the superb brake system taking care of repeated hard usage.

Even before it was announced, the 944 Turbo had competed in a 24-hour race in America. Porsche specialists Jim Busby, Rick Knoop and Freddy Baker had entered a prototype in the Nelson Ledges, Ohio, race the previous summer and strolled to victory 42 laps clear of their opposition! In yet another demonstration endurance specialist Gerhard Plattner had driven a 944 Turbo over a distance of 30,000 miles (50,000 kilometres) in 33 days, all on German highways (mostly *Autobahnen*). The car was fully-equipped with emission controls and was sometimes filled with 95 octane unleaded fuel, rather than 'super' without any appreciable loss of performance. By now, knock control had become extremely sophisticated with a sensor able to retard the ignition on any one plug.

To achieve high speeds in the 911 Carrera one has to concentrate fully. It is very rewarding to drive but rarely relaxing. The 944 Turbo, on the other hand,

Left *A completely new fascia design was introduced for the 944 Turbo, though also installed in the 944. It featured 928-style instruments and banished the last remnants of VW-Audi allegiance.*

Right and below *Careful attention to aerodynamics was important for the 944 Turbo, and included another frontal treatment plus a 'tray' at the back, to clean up the under-car airflow. With a flush-fitted windscreen, the drag coefficient was lowered to 0.33.*

The Porsche Turbo Cup series introduced in 1986 was enormously popular when launched, and went international the following year. The first series winner was Joachim Winkelock.

offered virtually the same performance without making any demands on the driver or passengers. Given a clear and unrestricted road it will rush effortlessly to an indicated 137 mph (220 km/h), or even to its maximum of 153 mph (245 km/h) with full throttle opening. To ease back on the throttle then hardly affects the running speed, but reduces the sound to a level usually associated with about half the speed! Wind noise, such as it is, is a rustle around the exterior mirror, and the road noise was markedly reduced too, thanks to the new subframe carriers. Now, the 944 and Turbo would treat pot-holes with disdain, even in the corners, and criticism would be correspondingly muted.

The 944 Turbo model, with catalysor, was put through the most stringent test in 1986 when a German national one-make racing series was organized. No fewer than 40 competitors took part in the six-race series which was extremely closely-fought, and Joachim Winkelhock was the worthy series winner. The cars had standard 220 bhp engines but roll cages were installed, trim and sound-deadening could be removed to cut the weight, a plastic engine cover was allowed, the suspension was lowered and Bilstein adjustable shock absorbers fitted.

Porsche sold the Turbo Cup model, ready to race, for DM78,900, and later offered the sport suspension package as a customer option, for the road. In 1987 the series was extended to ten races in Germany, Belgium and Italy (France organized its own series for cars without catalysors) and competitors were

Above In 1986 the Porsche Turbo Cup cars had standard catalyzed engines, rated at 220 bhp, but in 1987 the permitted power was raised to 250 bhp, and competitors were obliged to race with ABS brake equipment.

Below A full house into the first turns at the Nürburgring, where 40 drivers competed in the opening round of the Porsche Turbo Cup (Photo: Bilstein).

Left *Porsche offered fully-prepared cars for the Turbo Cup at DM78,900 apiece, equipment including sport suspension, Recaro seating for the driver and roll-bars.*

Below right *Two new versions of the 944 were announced at the end of 1987. Just 1,000 examples of a special edition 944 Turbo Sport were made, with 250 bhp, based on the Turbo Cup Championship car specification.*

allowed to raise the power to 250 bhp. The use of the new ABS braking system became mandatory, indicating Porsche's confidence in the system. Competitors regularly used the widest wheels in the options range, 8J × 16 in (40.5 cm) at the front and 9J × 16 in (40.5 cm) at the rear.

With or without emission equipment, the 944 Turbo could accelerate from rest to 60 mph inside six seconds while the important 100 mph figure (important to non-metric nations, anyway!) was achieved in 14.9 seconds. . . very little slower than the original 3-litre 911 Turbo. The 924 model, to which the 944 Turbo owed its origin, seemed a lifetime ago.

There was still one more model to come from Porsche's armoury, the 16-valve 944S. The engine had been previewed in the cabriolet study in September 1985 and it was formally announced a year later in a model that had most of the Turbo's features. Introduced at the same time of year as the 928S-4, this was the closest yet to combining the same technical elements of bore, stroke, pistons, cylinder head and twin overhead camshaft valvegear.

The 944S was, in fact, a half-way house between the 944 and the Turbo model in terms of power and performance, with a power output of 190 bhp and a maximum speed of 142 mph (227 km/h). The most important feature of all was its ability to achieve this power with or without three-way emission equipment, since the two-valve 944 model dropped to 150 bhp when the catalysor was installed and generally disappointed the German and American customers.

The four-valve head technology had already been applied to the US version 928S, and was about to be announced for the world-market 928S-4. The exhaust camshaft remained in its normal position, though driven by a heavier double-sided cogged belt, and a short chain, with a tensioner, was devised to drive the inlet valve camshaft. The camshafts had slightly higher profiles than in the 928S-4 in order to enhance performance at the top end and while the torque figure increased from 161 lb/ft (22.4 mkg) at 3,000 rpm to 181 lb/ft (25 mkg), it was achieved at 4,300 rpm. In this respect alone, the four-cylinder and eight-cylinder heads are not identical.

Paul Hensler explains that the complication and cost of the double camshaft layout was introduced purely and simply to meet emission requirements in the two most important markets, America and Germany, and any others such as Japan, Austria and Switzerland which adopted similar specifications. 'Our specific engine output was well out in front with two-valve heads, so long as we could use leaded fuel and no catalytic converter. We just didn't need the extra complication which four valves inevitably require. . . In today's world the catalytic converter engine is our baseline, and we don't believe customers should sacrifice performance when they choose to aid the environment. The goal became equal—or even more—power, with or without the converter.'

With a central spark plug location the 944S has the desired short flame travel, and four vertical valves offered the advantage of improved filling from a larger total intake cross-section. The shape of the combustion chamber was necessarily revised, manifolds and passages improved (the inlet manifold was made of magnesium) and the Motronic engine management system reprogrammed.

The 944S engine's compression ratio was raised from 10.6:1 to 10.9:1, a triple sensor knock control system introduced (enabling the engine to run on 91 octane fuel, if absolutely necessary, without being damaged), and the maximum engine speed limit was raised from 6,500 rpm to 6,800 rpm.

Gear ratios were raised, in line with the Turbo's, and apart from allowing higher speeds commensurate with the extra power, this also provided a bonus in fuel consumption.

While ABS was introduced to the 944 Turbo as standard equipment, it was offered as an option on the 944 and 944S and required new geometry at the front, with negative scrub and stronger spring leg rods. The wheels were given more offset and the so-called 'telephone dial' wheels were adopted as standard equipment.

Visually the 944S was distinguished from the 944 only by a discreet badge at the rear, and by '16 ventiler' script badges on the sides. It was not much to show for the extra money, and although the 16-valve model was aligned in pricing

much closer to the 944 than the Turbo, public reaction was not all that Porsche hoped for.

According to all the data available the 944S should be at least as powerful as the eight-valve up to 3,000 rpm, but no advantage was detectable, and in fact some testers felt that the eight-valve was a better bet. No-one disputed the extra power, but in markets not subject to emission controls this was evident only from 4,000 rpm through to the limit of 6,800 rpm, a realm which could only be explored in defiance of legal limits.

As Peter Schutz said, the reaction of the market to the 944S surprised and disappointed the company, although this applied to a lesser extent in the markets that mattered, America and Germany, when the catalyst equipment was installed. Then, a back-to-back with the 944 catalyst really did show some benefit.

Acceleration from rest to 100 km/h was marginally better, according to Porche's figures, at 7.9 seconds (8.4 seconds for the eight-valve), yet in Britain

Motor recorded 7.8 seconds for 0-60 mph, certainly a disappointing figure; the same journal established a top speed of 138 mph (220 km/h), rather less than Porsche's claim of 142 mph (227 km/h).

Not all of Porsche's new models are guaranteed instant success, and it would need only a few subtle changes to enhance the bottom-end performance of the 16-valve model, perhaps in gearing, valve timing or Motronic programming. These days Porsche is a listening company, and is bound to do whatever is necessary. Then again, the 944S was launched at the start of a difficult era as the German mark strengthened against most foreign currencies. Prices rocketed in America and Britain, the two most important export territories, and the Stuttgart company began to experience one of its cyclical recessions. Even in

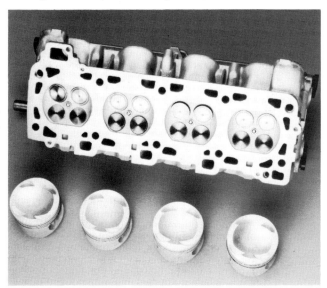

The 924S (above left) and 944S engine bays reveal major differences, though the 2.5-litre four-cylinder engine is basically the same. The 944S has a twin-cam, 16-valve cylinder head. The inlet manifold is made of cast magnesium, like that of the 928S-4.

Right and below *The 16-valve cylinder head of the 944S allows a central placing for each spark plug, and the pistons are bowled and indented. A short chain from the exhaust camshaft drives the inlet cam.*

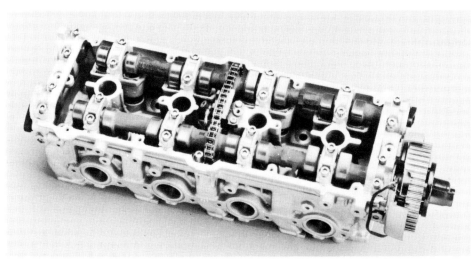

Britain, where Porsche is traditionally strong, price increases of 30 per cent in one calendar year, 1986, cannot be regarded as anything but bad news, and in 1987 sales dipped for the first time in 10 years, to the 3,000 mark.

The major part of the current four-cylinder programme is now complete, save for the official debut of the cabriolet version in 1988, but a hint at the future can be seen by privileged visitors to the Weissach reception centre. There is a cutaway 944 with three leading features: extensive use of HSLA (high strength light alloy) steel bodywork, a two-stage progressive turbo-charger, and PDK semi-automatic transmission. We have discussed the advantages of weight saving, and that is evidently a priority in the development programme.

In 1988 the 944 cabriolet is to be introduced, widening the appeal of the 4-cylinder series. Tony Lapine's styling department at Weissach is responsible for the classic changes to the rear bodywork.

4

Porsche's first V8: the 928

The first records of discussion about the 911's stable-mate, and possible successor, date back to 1968 but serious planning was begun in 1971 when (as mentioned earlier) Helmuth Bott conducted a detailed study of the various feasibilities and options.

A summary of the conclusion is that the next Porsche sports car would have a water-cooled engine at the front, and that the rear wheels would be driven by a rear-mounted trans-axle gearbox, either manual or automatic. Dr Ernst Fuhrmann, the newly-appointed managing director, approved the general layout on his birthday, 21 October 1971. Despite the apparent difficulties in solving problems of vibration in the long torque-tube shaft to the rear, this line of investigation was pursued on the grounds that a trans-axle would allow ideal weight distribution, a key factor in good handling.

The 928 would be larger than any Porsche built before, and—as had happened in the 911's gestation—the question arose as to whether it should be a four-seater. The answer was the same; that Porsche builds sports cars and would not become involved in any 'war' with Mercedes and BMW whose production volume, ten times greater, would make the outcome inevitable.

Some promising designs started to appear from Tony Lapine's studio in January 1972 and in February several 1:5 scale models were ready for inspection and testing in the wind tunnel. Paul Hensler's engine department, meanwhile, was proceeding with the design of a wide-angle V8 engine which would be unusually low, of 5-litre capacity and likely to develop 300 bhp. It would be constructed in aluminium alloy with a 90° 'vee' and would have a single overhead camshaft on each bank, driven by cogged belts rather than chains (apart from modernity, the chain tensioners were a continuing source of trouble to 911 owners).

The first test vehicle was a Mercedes 350 SL, original except for the installation of a trans-axle system 'borrowed' from the 908 racing car, with a rear-mounted clutch. Early trials were disappointing, as the clutch plates were difficult to clamp together, and as anticipated the torque tube, ¾ in (20 mm) in diameter and 6 ft 6 in (2 metres) in length, produced unwanted vibration. The system was then revised using the original Mercedes clutch, behind the engine, by

Left and below left *An Opel Commodore (coded V2) and an Audi Coupé (V4) were used to test the 928's systems, from 1972. The Opel was made wider, to accommodate the V8 engine, and was later adapted to develop the 'Weissach axle' design.*

Below right *Unlike anything produced before by Porsche, the 928 model surprised many visitors to the Geneva Show in March 1977, and shocked a few. The wide V8 engine fills the lateral space of the compartment although, thanks to the trans-axle, it is located well back behind the axle line. Seating is more generous than in the 911, but it is still a 2+2.*

increasing the torque tube diameter to 1 in (25 mm) and by replacing the three equidistant bearings with two larger ones, at the front and rear. The result was completely satisfactory, and could be further refined for production.

The next working prototype was V2, an Opel Admiral built to test suspension layouts, and it was this car that helped to perfect the patented 'Weissach axle' rear suspension, with variable geometry to correct oversteer tendencies if the throttle has to be released midway through a corner.

The pace of development quickened in 1973. In January the first V8 engine, with carburettors, ran for the first time, but ground to a halt within minutes with water pouring out of the crankcase. This was strengthened for a further trial in March, and strengthened again for the definitive test in May, when it started a 250-hour endurance test (it was run for 209 hours on full load). It was equipped with Bosch K-Jetronic fuel injection.

An Audi 100 Coupé became V3, a vehicle rebuilt on the 928's floorpan and equipped with the V8 engine, trans-axle system and anticipated suspension design. It was built in September 1973 and completed a major endurance trial in Algeria in November, immediately prior to a meeting of the supervisory board and the board of management. It was a difficult, even critical meeting, because the supervisory board did not unanimously approve all the work completed and it was reviewed in the light of the Middle East war that had just broken out between Egypt and Israel. Equally worrying, there was a strong lobby in Germany againt sports cars, in fact against any cars, as the Greens movement began to emerge, and Dr Fuhrmann expressed the opinion that Projekt 928 might be a good one, 'but we must ask ourselves whether it is the right product now.'

Intensive development was suspended for 12 months as the world came to grips with oil shortages and soaring prices. Most attention at Weissach now turned to the EA 425 project (Porsche 924) due for launch in 1975, and anything done to the 928 was of a defensive nature. The V8 engine was reduced to 3.9-litre capacity and tested with carburettors, but the performance was so poor that it was realized that it would be completely inadequate with American emission equipment applied.

In particular the rear suspension was still not performing satisfactorily. V2, the Opel Admiral, was redesigned with torsion bars, a favourite Porsche system, replacing coil springs, and an extra steering wheel was located between the front seats so that a man sitting in the back could alter the toe-in of the rear wheels, an active test of the Weissach system. Not until the end of 1975, when four actual 928 prototypes had been built, tested and approved by the board, was the eventual solution found, and it involved complex geometry and bushing development, with a control link that allowed the outer rear wheel to toe-out when power was diminished. This eliminated the car's natural tendency to tuck-in, with the potential to spin, and it became one of the most highly-praised of all the 928's safety features.

In July 1976 the sixth (W-6) 928 prototype was built with all the model's leading features including an engine capacity of 4.5-litres, now approved for production, and the patent 'Weissach axle' rear suspension layout. The last prototype, W-12, was built in March 1977 even as the 928 was launched publicly at the Geneva Show, and the first O-Series production cars went down the line at Zuffenhausen, where a completely new building had been prepared.

At first the 928 drew mixed comment, for it looked unusually wide for its overall length, and the arrangement of the headlamps, open and facing skyward

Above *The headlamps were considered one of the least atttractive features of the 928, exposed to the sky in daytime.*

Below *Although rather short for its width, the 928 looked a powerful machine right from the start. Quiet at high speed, it was an ideal long-distance car for two people with plenty of luggage.*

An early styling concept (**right**) *envisaged a sharp-fronted coupé with elongated side glass and a conventional rear hatch; this sketch would date to early 1972. By autumn 1973 a full-size plasticine model shows the 928's characteristics clearly, although covered headlamps are still a possibility.*

Below *Stylist Anatole Lapine won his case to have the headlamps exposed, as a way of accentuating the length of the bodywork. The comparatively narrow engine lid serves the same purpose.*

Left *The 928 model, with Porsche's 4.5-litre V8 engine, took the Stuttgart company into a completely new field. It was large and luxurious, but offered the traditional sporting characteristics. It immediately won the international Car Of The Year award.*

Below *The Porsche 911 Carrera. The sport equipment wing may be a 'plus', but most customers choose the traditional-style Fuchs alloy wheels.*

Bottom *The first cabriolet was prepared by Helmuth Bott at Weissach in 1980, and Peter Schutz gave the go-ahead for the model which went on sale in 1982.*

Almost 'square' in length, width and height, the 928's 90° V8 engine featured an interesting Bosch K-Jetronic injection manifold system and had hydraulic tappets, which were maintenance free.

in the daytime, reminded people of something on a fishmonger's slab! With a wheelbase of 98.4 in (2,500 mm), the 928 was 175 in (4,447 mm) in length and 72.6 in (1,836 mm) in width. . . plus another 10 in (250 mm) for two exterior mirrors.

The width of the engine, 29.6 in (752 mm) dictated the size of the engine bay, and space then had to be allowed for the front wheels, at least 7 in (178 mm) in width, to be turned to full lock. Designer Lapine really had no choice in the overall sizing of the model, though in pure terms he would have preferred it to be longer and therefore better proportioned. Stylists were not consulted on matters such as this, however. To minimize the stumpy looks he chose to expose the headlamps to distract the eye of the beholder, and make the bonnet opening fairly narrow, tapering to the front.

The engine itself, unusually 'square' with a length of 33.9 in (860 mm) and a height of merely 28.0 in (710 mm) weighed 520 lb (236 kg) less clutch, starter and oil, otherwise ready for installation. At 4,474 cc it developed 240 bhp at 5,250 rpm and 267.5 lb/ft (37 mkg) of torque at 3,600 rpm, equipped with Bosch K-Jetronic injection and having a compression ratio of 8.5:1. At the rear of the long torque tube was either a new Porsche five-speed transmission or a three-speed automatic made by Daimler-Benz. The manual version was unusual in having a twin-plate clutch, each 7⅞ in (200 mm) in diameter in the interests of compactness, with hydraulic control.

All aluminium in construction, with a high silicon content, the engine featured hydraulic tappets for the valves, and these maintained their clearances for life; contactless ignition was something else that could be ignored at the

Left *The trans-axle system had already proved itself in the 924 model and, with a rather frail twin-plate clutch behind the engine, would endow the 928 with excellent weight distribution. Mounting battery box on the trans-axle finally cured vibration problems.*

Left *The instrument nacelle would tilt with the steering wheel, and the layout was highly praised. Air conditioning even extended to the glove box!*

Below left *It took four years of patient development to perfect the Weissach rear axle design, which allowed the outer rear wheel to toe-out under deceleration when loaded.*

Right *The entire drivetrain is offered up to the suspended 928 body during production, facilitating assembly. Made entirely of galvanized steel, aluminium or composites, the 928 is virtually corrosion-free.*

20,000 kilometre service intervals, and the battery, also maintenance-free, was completely hidden in the well of the luggage compartment, its carrier attached to the back of the gearbox. This was the last step, and one of the more important, in eliminating completely unwanted vibration from the transmission.

The 928's body structure was made of galvanized steel, the doors, wings and engine cover of aluminium, while the moulded front and rear body sections, which concealed shock-absorber mounted beams, were made of flexible polyurethane material (the development of paint that would deform and recover took longer to develop than the actual mouldings).

There was, therefore, no component in the 928 that could corrode—even the brake lines were made of non-corroding steel, and in theory a ten-year-old model 928 could be as good as a new one, allowing for wear and tear.

There were many features for the public to admire at the Geneva Show. The height of the headlamp beams could be adjusted by means of a knob beside the

driver's seat; if optional air-conditioning was fitted, even the glove box could be cooled; a comprehensive warning system was incorporated with 12 vital functions wired in, before such systems became fashionable; the 19-gallon (86-litre) fuel tank was moulded in a special plastic, to fit exactly the floor under the luggage compartment, and featuring a recess for the space-saver spare wheel; the rack and pinion steering had variable rate assistance, and the four brake discs were fully ventilated, and gripped by floating callipers (Porsche claimed, rather optimistically, that they were fade-free and the brake fluid temperature would never exceed 90°C).

The wheels were 16 in (40.5 cm) in diameter, made of cast alloy, and were equipped with 225/60 VR 16 tyres, usually Pirelli P7 though Goodyear NCTs and Dunlop D4 tyres were later introduced.

There was no doubt that the world's press admired the Porsche 928, the more so after driving the car in the Alpes Maritimes in southern France. The 928

could accelerate to 62 mph (100 km/h) in under seven seconds, cover the standing kilometre in 27 seconds, and had a maximum speed of 143 mph (230 km/h). It was extremely refined (comment about road rumble would come later, with the full tests) and handled like no other luxury car; in fact it was hard to think of a competitor. Effortless steering, yet with plenty of feel, and above all the inherently safe characteristics of the Weissach axle, were highly praised.

Orders flooded in for the 928, far in excess of the number of cars that could be built. In Britain there were three applicants for every car that was expected in the 1979 model year, deliveries of right-hand drive models scheduled for September, and at £19,500 it was realistically priced, at £3,000 more than the Jaguar XJ-S model. That included air-conditioning and part leather upholstery, though the optional chequered seat velours were fairly hard on the eye.

The ultimate accolade was the International Car of the Year award, a European-based ballot of leading motoring writers. The result, a clear-cut

Left *A well-equipped and spacious hall was built at Zuffenhausen, to produce the 928 model.*

Right *As with the 911's six-cylinder engines, the 8-cylinder is hand-assembled, then dyno tested, before being mated to the trans-axle tube.*

success for the 928 over a whole range of family saloons, came as a considerable surprise to Porsche's management, which supposed that the 928 would finish lower in the order on account of its price and exclusivity.

It was the proudest day of Dr Fuhrmann's life when he travelled to Monte Carlo in January 1978, to receive the award from Prince Rainier. Adding to his pleasure, a privately-owned Porsche 911 had driven into the Principality as winner of the Monte Carlo Rally.

The 928 represented an investment of DM200 million, twice the 'cut price' cost of the 924 although it would have been even greater without the four-cylinder model, which made its contribution to trans-axle development. From the start, the 928 would be produced at a rate of 5,000 per annum, or 21 per working day, and that rate varied very little in the next ten years. At the time of the 928's launch it was priced at DM55,000 on the German market, the 911 cost DM38,000 and the 924 cost DM24,000, representing a good cross-section of the sports car ownership spectrum.

The original plan, back in 1974, was to price the 928 model about 10 per cent higher than the 911, and the 928S version at 10 per cent above the 911 Carrera. Clearly this scenario had slipped very badly since the 928, realistically priced, was a full 31 per cent dearer than the 911 and stood no chance at all of being the six-cylinder model's replacement. This fact alone caused some acrimonious

In February 1978, a month after the Car of the Year accolade, Austrians Rudi Lins and Gerhard Plattner undertook a marathon proving trial form New York to Moscow, and Paris, visiting the Arctic Circle on both continents.

At 4.7-litres, and 300 horsepower, the 928S was still not quite the high-performing model that Dr Fuhrmann intended, but it pleased the customers.

boardroom discussion, sales director Schmidt caught between Dr Fuhrmann, whose reputation depended on the eight-cylinder, and Dr Porsche who was distinctly antagonistic. Dr Fuhrmann set in motion a plan to strip out the 928 to reduce its price but this, historically, was bound to be a loser and won him no new friends.

In February 1978 those intrepid Austrians, Rudi Lins and Gerhard Plattner, achieved one of their marathons in the 928 covering more than 17,360 miles (28,000 kilometres) in 33 days. Their route took them from New York across the American continent to San Francisco, then up the west coast all the way to Fairbanks, Alaska, before turning east to Montreal, and an airlift to Europe. Then from Frankfurt the 928 headed for Rovaneimi in the Arctic Circle, Helsinki, Moscow, Warsaw and Berlin, all achieved without mechanical problems. The cold, though, was intense, down to -60°C in places, but the car never needed digging out of snow.

The first, in fact the only real development on the 4.5-litre 928 came at the same time as the announcement of the 4.7-litre 928S, just before the start of the 1979 model year. Like the more powerful version, the 928's compression ratio was raised to 10:1 and this, coupled with careful recalibration of ignition and fuel injection, resulted in fuel savings of between 15 and 20 per cent at different speeds, though premium fuel with a 97 octane rating was required.

The torque figure rose from 260 to 280 lb/ft (36 to 39 mkg) still at 3,600 rpm, but the power rating of 240 bhp didn't change at all, apparently because not all

Above *The majority of eight-cylinder Porsches, up to 90 per cent in some markets, are sold with Daimler-Benz automatic transmission, now a four-speed. With power to spare the automatic versions are pleasant and easy to drive. To the right of the seat is the headlamp beam height adjustment control.*

Left *Just how far back in the chassis lies the V8 engine can be seen in this shot, the mass being behind the front axle line. A viscous coupling fan was used until 1986.*

production engines actually reached that figure. . . now they did, and the 928 became noticeably faster in acceleration.

Not all owners, especially the aggressive press-on types who had previously owned 911s, agreed that the braking system was above reproach, and the 'S' version's thicker discs and larger pads were quietly introduced to the specification, obviating criticism.

In 1981 the anti-corrosion warranty was extended to seven years, and 12 months later there were minor changes that included improved interior ventilation, the flow rate being increased by 10 per cent. Then in the summer of 1982, the 4.5-litre model was withdrawn from the range as demand for the series 2 928S kept the production workers busy.

_____Fuel-saving_____

It was typical of Dr Fuhrmann's thinking that the world was against sports cars in some way, and the bigger, faster and more thirsty they were, the greater would be the resistance to them. He was correct to the extent that greater fuel economy is always desirable; even if the owner can well afford to fill the tank, he likes to be able to tell all his acquaintances how he can drive from Stuttgart to Berlin or from London to Edinburgh without stopping for fuel!

It must have been something approaching paranoia that caused the development of the 'part-time' V8 engine at Weissch, and journalists were invited there in the summer of 1979 to see and drive not only the TOP 924 models, but a 928 which ran on only four cylinders at urban speeds. Not only that, but the engine would also stop itself when the car had idled for a few seconds, and would restart when the accelerator was depressed.

In effect the part-time 928 had a pair of four-cylinder engines, each with its own fuel injection and ignition system, throttle butterfly and inlet manifold. The pairings were of alternate cylinders so that balance would be maintained, and with a small throttle opening four would operate normally and four would idle, with the advantage of higher loads, and better thermal efficiency, of those in operation. Full throttle opening, and a speed in excess of 74 mph (120 km/h), brought the four idling cylinders smoothly into operation.

In the urban cycle the 928's consumption improved by nearly 15 per cent, from 15.8 mpg (17 litres/100 km) to 18.1 mpg (15.6 litres/100 km), while at a steady 56 mph (90 km/h) it improved by 13 per cent, from 21.4 mpg (13 litres/100 km) to 24.2 mpg (11.6 litres/100 km), though at 75 mph (120 km/h) there was hardly any difference. Such a solution was admitted to be very expensive, but Paul Hensler pointed out that the study also allowed the possibility of having two separate engines under the bonnet, one tuned for torque and the other for power, using different exhaust pipe lengths, different manifolds and even different camshaft profiles.

The development was regarded mainly as a safety net, in case demand for the 928 slackened very badly. It did not, and so the project was shelved in 1981.

In parallel, Helmuth Flegl conducted a study of the sports car of the future,

In 1980 Porsche showed the unique 960 model at Frankfurt, considerably lighter than a normal 928 but safer in impacts. In the top picture, the right side of the chassis has been subjected to a 37 mph impact, which was absorbed by twin tubular structures. The rear bumper consisted of wound fibreglass reinforced material.

his 'project 995' appearing in clay form in 1979. It was not unlike the 928, but the bulbous look had been replaced by a more svelte and windcheating shape which combined practicality with a Cd figure of 0.3. It was a four-seater with a high degree of active and passive safety, incorporating such things as lead-time steering, ABS braking, a PDK gearbox, electronic throttle control and electronic wheelspin control, the latter feature adopted by Volvo in 1985.

Two power units were envisaged, a 2.2-litre four cylinder and a 3-litre V8, both capable of meeting certain performance targets: 0-60 mph acceleration in under 10 seconds, a maximum speed of at least 124 mph (200 km/h), a cruising range of at least 300 miles (480 km), and an average fuel economy of at least 30 mpg (9 litres/100 km). Flegl rejected a diesel engine on the grounds that in meeting the performance target, it would be so large in capacity that it could not meet the fuel consumption, and would be too noisy. Noise control also featured prominently in Flegl's study, as did weight. The entire body and chassis would be constructed in aluminium as a means of keeping the kerb weight below 2,860 lb (1,300 kg); such a structure would save around 220 lb (100 kg) compared with an all-steel monocoque, and the steel content would be no more than 40 per cent of the total weight, as against 22 per cent in the 936 racing car (the absolute minimum) and 51 per cent in the 928 production model.

The 995 was not built as a running model, but many of its lessons were incorporated in the Porsche 960 research study, a futuristic 928, shown at Frankfurt in September 1981. Elsewhere in the exhibition, on the Alusuisse/Alusingen stand, was a bare 928 bodyshell (designed and constructed at Weissach, in fact) made entirely of a new alloy named Anticorodal-120R. The shell, easily lifted by two men, weighed only 333 lb (151 kg) compared with 644 lb (292 kg) for an all-steel body, or 567 lb (257 kg) for the actual 928 production body using aluminium doors, wings and bonnet.

It was estimated that assuming an annual mileage of 21,700 miles (35,000 km) a German owner would save up to DM400 a year on fuel alone, and the car's performance would certainly be enhanced by a saving of 233 lb (106 kg). The 944 Turbo 'study' now at Weissach, made of similar HSLA alloy-steel, proves that development has continued and leaves no doubt at all that intensive weight-savings are high on Porsche's priority list.

On Porsche's own stand at Frankfurt, the 928-based 960 study incorporated the ideas of light bodywork and the 995's active and passive safety features. In addition to the usual aluminium contents the entire front of the car was made of the same lightweight material, which is half the weight of steel and four or five times more expensive. HSLA alloy-steel was used in the side structures, rear side panels, roof and rear lid, and the total vehicle weight was 2,405 lb (1,090 kg) which compared very favourably with the production 928's 3,197 lb (1,450 kg).

A total of 10.6 lb (4.8 kg) was saved in the front and rear bumpers alone, using wound fibreglass-reinforced material which could absorb two or three times more energy than steel or aluminium tubes. The trans-axle torque shaft, too, was made 32 per cent lighter by substituting fibreglass reinforced plastic for steel.

Careful design made the 960 safer in accidents, the wall impact speed, for

Inside the 960 was a specially designed child safety seat, bolted to the trans-axle. A heat-resisiting rear window is almost a necessity for people in the rear seats.

instance, being increased from 30 to 37 mph (48 to 59 km/h) for a given amount of damage; pedestrian injuries, too, would be reduced. Lateral and rear collision safety was improved as well, while inside the car the seats had built-in restraints (previewed in the 995), and head loads on impact would be reduced by 30-50 per cent. A specially-designed child seat offering a high degree of protection was bolted to the trans-axle tunnel at three points.

The front seats had their own hydro-pneumatic suspension, said to reduce the median vibration loads by half, and the damping was self-adjusting to allow for passenger weight, road surface and speed. The 960 also featured the Bosch/Porsche tyre pressure sensors, later incorporated in the 959 but already tested in Porsche's racing cars, on the premise that more than half the cars on the road run with pressures that are too low.

The 960's engine carried the TOP principle further with a compression of 12.5:1, with digital electronics to keep it under control, while the gearbox was a prototype of the PDK twin-clutch, semi-automatic system, then called PDG (Porsche Dual-clutch Gearbox).

_____S for satisfaction_____

In the summer of 1979, for the 1980 model year, Porsche announced the 4.7-litre 928S. It was the version that the company would have preferred to introduce from the outset, except for the planned 5-litre engine, and was warmly welcomed by customers who had felt almost cheated as they parted with 911s while feeling that the 4.5-litre 928 lacked muscle.

The 928S *did* have muscle, developing 300 bhp at 5,900 rpm with infinitely more sporting characteristics. Higher compression at 10:1, larger valves, higher lift camshafts and reduced back-pressure in the exhaust system all contributed to a healthy growl that the 4.5-litre did not have, and a far more satisfying range of acceleration. *Motor* reported a 0-60 mph acceleration time of 6.2 seconds (7.0 for the 4.5-litre), 14.2 seconds to 100 mph (17.8 seconds) and 22.1 seconds to 120 mph (31.3 seconds). The maximum speed was raised from 140 mph (224 km/h) to 156 mph (250 km/h), yet the fuel consumption figure of 16.0 mpg (17.6 litres/100 km) overall, compared with 14.9 mpg (18.9 litres/100 km) for the 4.5-litre in the hands of the same test staff. The 4.5-litre, in fairness, also had its compression raised to 10:1 at the same time and would be a more economical car still.

The greater engine capacity was achieved by increasing the bore dimension from 3¾ in (95 mm) to 3⅞ in (97 mm), the stroke remaining at 3 in (78.9 mm), and the actual capacity was 4,664 cc. Thicker brake discs and redesigned calipers, allowing a greater pad area, were also adopted for the 4.5-litre 928.

With the 25 per cent increase in power came a 10.3 per cent increase in torque, from 257 lbft (35.7 mkg) to 284 lbft (39.4 mkg), though higher up in the range at 4,500 rpm (the 1980 model 928, though, now developed 280 lbft (38.9 mkg) of torque at 3,600 rpm), and the maximum engine speed was raised from 6,200 rpm to 6,500 rpm. Despite all this, no changes were considered necessary for the suspension (still rated as rather harsh by the road-testers) or for the transmission.

Visually the 928S became a little more aggressive. A front air dam incorporated ducting to the front brakes, and in conjunction with a polyurethane spoiler around the back window the drag figure was reduced from 0.4 to 0.38, making its own contribution to the higher maximum speed. Body-coloured side rubbing-strips were standardized, stone-chipping resistance was improved along the doors and

In side view, at speed, the 928S looked absolutely right in proportions. The 'S' would accelerate to 100 mph in 14.2 seconds, quicker than the 911, and had a maximum speed of 156 mph.

At Nardo, a 928S covered 6,033 kilometres in 24 hours, in 1982. It was equipped, prior to the announcement, with the latest in Bosch LH-Jetronic injection equipment, and developed 310 bhp.

lower body panels, and finally a new type of slab-sided forged alloy wheel was introduced, still 16 in (40.5 cm) in diameter but equipped with Pirelli P7 tyres of 225/50 dimension.

The Porsche 928S has had a very limited competitions career, due mainly to the lack of support for the Group B (Grand Touring) category throughout the world. In 1982 Gerhard Plattner suggested a novel idea to the Porsche factory and ran a 928S for 24 hours at the Nardo proving ground in southern Italy. Plattner, with Peter Lovett and Peter Zbinden from the British and German Porsche dealer networks, took the 'Tirolean Eagle' flat-out around the 7.8 mile (12.6 km), slightly banked track and covered a total distance of 3,740 miles (6,033 km), at an average of 156.2 mph (250 km/h). The car was virtually in standard trim, except for a fairing under the engine, blanking off the brake cooling ducts (the brakes were needed only for pit stops every 32 laps, or 251 miles (405 km), and removing the windscreen wipers. Although it was not announced at the time, the record-breaker was also equipped with Bosch LH-Jetronic fuel injection and electronically-controlled ignition timing, features which helped raise the power output to 310 bhp.

In Britain, AFN Limited, a subsidiary of the Porsche factory and of PCGB, entered a 928S in the Uniroyal Production Sports Car Championship, and the open-exhaust, bellowing V8 became a firm favourite with the crowds. Between them, regular drivers Tony Dron and Tony Lanfranchi notched up eight victories, four second places and a third, and easily won Britain's only 24-hour race, for saloon and GT cars, at Snetterton. Again, the 928S was in near standard form, as the regulations insist, but with blueprinting the engine gave an estimated 330 bhp, and an actual 245 bhp at the rear wheels.

In 1984, German and French teams got bolder and ran a 928S in rounds of the World Endurance Championship, in the Group B category. The Porsche was, naturally, completely eclipsed by the 956 model, along with the Lancias, even by the 911 Turbos, and while the performances may have been worthy they were almost embarrassing to watch, and the factory was certainly not amused.

The 928 has never been regarded by the factory as suitable for competitions, but the British dealership AFN Limited campaigned one successfully in 1983, in the national production sports car series. Among the car's eight wins was success in the Snetterton 24-Hour race.

Such were the changes announced in 1983 for the 1984 model year that PCGB had the new model named Series 2, and had that painted on the tail. Most significantly, the Bosch LH Jetronic system was more efficient, using the new heated wire process for measuring the mass of air, rather than the flow, as it entered the induction system. It allowed even more precise injection control, better engine flexibility and lower emissions, and in conjunction with electronic ignition control the power output was raised from 300 to 310 bhp. Torque was also increased, from 284 lbft (39.2 mkg) to 295 lbft (40.77 mkg), and as a result the S2's maximum speed was raised to 158 mph (253 km/h), while the 0-60 mph time was reduced by half a second.

Daimler-Benz's new four-speed automatic transmission introduced closer, and much more suitable ratios and transformed the performance, the 0-60 mph figure reduced from 7.0 seconds to 6.5 seconds, and the maximum speed rose to 152 mph (243 km/h). Nor surprisingly perhaps, 70 per cent of customers world-wide chose the automatic version in the 1984 model year.

Even with this higher performance, fuel economy was improved by 10 per cent overall, most markedly at steady speeds of 56 mph (90 km/h) and 75 mph (120 km/h); at 75 mph (120 km/h) the consumption was 27.7 mpg (10 litres/100 km) instead of 22.1 mpg (12.5 litres/100 km), an improvement of 25 per cent.

On the subject of ABS braking, Porsche's sales director Lars-Roger Schmidt was fond of saying 'Those who need it most have it first.' The fact was that the Weissach engineers were not happy with the first generation system, which could be badly caught out by a series of heavy applications, and worked hard with Bosch to develop the second generation, which became standard equipment and incorporated a three-channel, four-sensor system, split front to rear.

On the comfort side, the seats were redesigned to allow more headroom (which had been critical, if electrically operated seats were specified in conjunction with an electric sunroof), new materials were introduced, and a very sophisticated Blaupunkt Atlanta stereo radio/cassette system installed as standard; many owners found the radio's manual to be more complex than the car's! The boot lid could now be released by catches on either side of the interior, facilitating passenger operation, a door central locking system button was placed on the centre console, the steering wheel was now fully adjustable, for reach as well as rake, and Goodyear NCT and Dunlop D4 tyres were introduced as alternatives to Pirelli P7 equipment.

It was at this time, in 1983, that the decision was made to cease development of engines requiring leaded fuel; all future power units would be developed to produce equal power with, or without catalysors, primarily for the benefit of American customers who, according to Schutz, were treated like second-class citizens, but not least with an eye to forthcoming European regulations.

For the first time in Porsche's history a new model, exclusive at first to the American market, was launched in America in January 1985. It was called the 928S like its predecessor, but at Weissach it is referred to as the series 3, and it was powered by a heavily-revised engine. With the bore taken out to the full 4 in (100 mm), the same as the 944, the capacity was raised to 4,957 cc, and on each bank was a pair of camshafts driving four valves per cylinder.

As already described for the 944S, the exhaust valve cams were left in position and a short chain, with tensioner, was carried across to drive the inlet camshafts, the solution also chosen by VW for the Golf 16-valve model.

The compression ratio was raised from 9.03 to 10:1, and the power graph was completely transformed from a rather gutless 234 bhp to 288 bhp. The maximum speed of the catalyzed, automatic model went up from 143 mph (229 km/h) to 155 mph (248 km/h), and the 0-60 mph time tumbled from 6.8 seconds to 6.1 seconds.

That the 48-valve 928S could exceed America's national speed limit by 100 mph (160 km/h) was of no concern to the clientele. It was to them what the 928S had been to the 4.5-litre 928 in 1979, and it had taken a long time in coming. Fuel consumption was improved at the same time, and the price tag of $50,000 seemed quite reasonable when set against other European 'supercars' which could not match the performance in catalyzed form.

This was now the jewel of PCNA's range, for the Turbo had been withdrawn from the market in 1980 and did not return there until 1986 when the latest techniques in emission control had been applied. Peter Schutz also mentioned that this, and other 'world models' with equal performance, would eliminate the troublesome 'grey market' in private imports, for up to 25 per cent of Porsches sold in Germany found their way to America and, with the minimum of work to comply with exhaust regulations, found eager buyers. In particular, German Porsche dealers were sick of having their used-car showrooms cleared of low mileage models by agents for the American market. 'It is easy to sell these cars at good prices, but the buyers do not become customers,' complained Cologne dealer Erwin Kremer. 'I never see those cars again in my workshop, and I never have enough cars for my personal customers.' His concern was shared by many others.

For Porsche, this was still only a half-way house to the world model; American and Japanese customers had all the benefits of twin-cam technology, Germans and other Europeans did not. In the summer of 1986 the S3 was replaced, after

The new polyurethane front-end treatment of the 928S-4 combined the spot, fog and turn lamps in units, and contributed to the lower drag figure of 0.34. The S-4 was smoother underneath and an electrically-operated 'venetian blind' metered the amount of intake air.

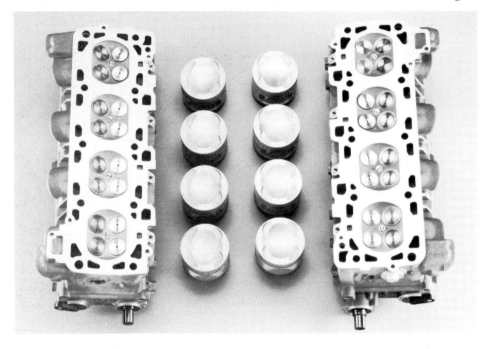

a short life, by the S4 which was to be sold with identical engine performance in every country in the world. This, too, had the full 5-litre capacity and the S3's double camshaft layout, but it now developed 320 bhp with, or without catalysor. For non-catalyst markets this represented a jump of 10 bhp, but for the Americans and Japanese it represented a second power-rise in 20 months, by a further 32 bhp. On the other side of the equation, the price was raised by a full 20 per cent to DM120,000 on the German market, and with the Deutschmark appreciating daily against the dollar and the pound, importers pursed their lips pensively.

Visually the 928S-4 changed quite a lot for the better. A new and very aero-dyanamic polyurethane nose fairing incorporated sleeker fog, driving and indicator lamps, and the air dam was made deeper. Attention was paid to under-body drag, and at the rear the small spoiler around the tailgate opening was replaced by a larger aerodynamic wing, a device that was hinged and could tilt upwards (otherwise, explained the engineers, owners would have problems in the car-wash).

The drag factor was now reduced from 0.38 to 0.34, a major improvement which contributed heavily to the car's top speed of 168 mph (269 km/h), or 165 mph (264 km/h) in automatic form, and Al Holbert, Porsche's motorsport director in America, took a 928S-4 down the Bonneville salt flats at 171 mph (274 km/h) to prove the point, in standard trim apart from the 'Nardo' refine-ments of removing wipers and blanking off the brake ducts. That the 928S-4 could do all this with negative lift, or downforce in other words, was a tribute to the aerodynamic work done in the scale wind tunnel for while others might

Similar, but not identical to the 944S cylinder head, the 928S-4 adopted the twin-cam layout at the same time, in 1986. The S3 version for America had tested the layout in the previous 20 months. Now, the benefits of similarity between 4 and 8-cylinder designs would pay off handsomely.

see better drag figures, they did not have the downforce.

Taking thermal efficiency and aerodynamic drag research to its ultimate stage, a 'venetian blind' cowling was fitted in front of the radiator. The angle of the blades was varied by an electric servo motor, operated in turn by electronics sensitive to ambient temperature, engine temperature and speed. Research showed that 19 per cent of driving is at urban speed, when the flaps are fully open (then the Cd figure is 0.352, but that is of no consequence). Some 59 per cent of average driving is at medium speeds up to 80 mph (130 km/h) and then the blind is 30 per cent open, resulting in a drag figure of 0.343, while the remaining 22 per cent of driving is at motorway speeds and then the flaps are fully closed, the Cd figure being 0.34. The radiator was now cooled by a pair of electric fans, replacing a large, single viscous coupled fan. Another thoughtful touch, the windscreen wiper arms were set ¾ in (20 mm) lower, to reduce drag and to improve visibility.

In transmission, a single clutch of 9⅞ in (250 mm) diameter replaced the rather weak pair of 7⅞ in (200 mm) clutches, and the automatic's torque converter was increased in diameter from 10⅜ in (270 mm) to 11⅜ in (290 mm). Gear ratios were 'shortened' by 8 per cent in the automatic so that the maximum speed coincided with peak power, at 6,000 rpm, and the electronics were arranged to allow a half-second power 'lag' when upshifting, to iron out any possible jolts.

Of interest in the engine, which retained the Bosch LH Jetronic injection and 'mapped' electronic ignition, the intake manifold material was changed to magnesium and consisted of two chambers connected by a resonance tube. By alternating the pulses on each bank, the inlet air was set to vibrate at a frequency identical to pressure pulses in the enclosed intake distributor. This resulted in a charging effect, even at low speeds, which completed the cylinder filling with benefit to torque and general performance.

At a price, the 928S-4 became a technological marvel, the peak of production development, though not quite as futuristic as the 959 intended for merely 200 wealthy customers.

There are very few cars that can travel at faster speeds on the public highways, and none which can sustain extremely high speeds in serene comfort. I drove one on a derestricted *Autobahn* at the time of the launch and tested, just once on a clear road, the ease with which the speedometer needle would swing around to more than 160 mph (260 km/h), a speed which is really only suitable for a race track.

At more moderate speeds the 928S-4 glides along effortlessly, ready to surge through holes in traffic, accelerating with a muted but powerful growl from the V8 engine. The five-speed manual transmission was almost superfluous, acceleration being strong in the highest gear at 62 mph (100 km/h), and the automatic version was equally satisfying. The steady speed fuel consumption figures were actually better than the previous model's, the cost of the S-4 coming mainly as one big down-payment.

The brakes, with four-piston alloy callipers, are superbly capable of dealing with emergencies, and roadholding is enhanced by the use of wider wheels at the rear, with 8J rims, those at the front remaining at 7J section. An oversteering tendency had been noted in earlier models, at the limit, and this was now cured.

What further developments could there be? The 928S-4 is probably now as fast as it ever needs to be, though weight savings alone could make it faster, with

In 1984 full four-seat version of the 928S was presented to Professor Porsche on his 75th birthday. It was faithful to one of the concept designs in 1972 but featured 'bubble' headlamps, and previewed the S-4 frontal style.

Atop the subtly changed rear polyurethane body panel, a large wing is hinged to tilt upwards. Better for car washes, say the German engineers!

even better handling and more economical, and it is my guess that future developments will be along these lines. Porsche has already laid down a small series of 928s lightened by 265 lb (120 kg) by removing the air conditioning, the radio, much of the soundproofing and the electric seat adjustments, and by fitting a simplified (though still catalyzed) exhaust system.

The Club Sport model has 8J rims at the front, 9J rims at the rear, and runs with lowered suspension and stiffer (sport) shock absorbers. There are those who say that the 911 Carrera is the only model in the range that truly excites the owner. . . the 928S-4 Club Sport is guaranteed to have the same effect, though. Despite its simplified equipment, it is no less expensive than the luxury mainstream model, but that is no deterrent to those who buy Porsches mainly for their adrenalin value.

So is the four-seater concept really dead? A Porsche team led by senior engineer Richard Hetmann styled and produced a genuine four-seat 928S which was presented to Professor Porsche on his 75th birthday in 1984, and the styling was really very pleasing. A plate adding 10 in (25 cm) was inserted in the floorpan, extending the wheelbase and allowing proper space for adults in the rear seats. The B-pillar was redesigned and the roof line extended to improve headroom, turning the 928S into something more like an estate car.

The front wings were given a more pronounced 'crease' at the top, making them easier for the driver to see, and the headlamps were now cowled, taking away the fishy look. Professor Porsche's one-off 928S, which he likes very much, was the first to be equipped with a US-spec 5-litre, 32-valve engine which more than compensated for the extra weight (3,515 lb (1,625 kg) rather than 3,476 lb (1,580 kg)).

In the immediate future though, Porsche's attention will concentrate on further development of the six-cylinder models, in ways previewed in the 959.

5

The miracle car: the 911

Porsche's 911 model reached its 20th anniversary in 1984 with production nearing the quarter-million mark, an amazing figure for a sports car that was never inexpensive, and in Turbo form ranked among the world's finest super-cars. It succeeded the 356 as Porsche's pillar of existence, the model upon which the company's fame depended, yet it might have been phased out of production in the year of George Orwell's awful prediction but for a substantial change of policy that occurred in 1981.

Professor Porsche was absolutely correct in envisaging a strong demand for the six-cylinder model for many years to come, and Peter Schutz was his new, willing partner in seeing that development started again in the 1980s. More than anything else in the Zuffenhausen range it offered raw power and sheer joy in driving, allied with an increasing level of sophistication.

On price alone it could never have competed with the 'back to nature' MGs and Austin-Healeys, nor even the Jaguar E-types from which many customers graduated, but it became accepted as a success symbol for people who never lost their youth. The fact that the engine was hung behind the rear wheels, and demanded attentiveness from the driver in difficult circumstances, was also regarded as a virtue. Careful development over the years almost eliminated the tail-happy tricks of the original cars anyway, and the reward, always available, was the searing thrust of acceleration, and the unique boom of the 'boxer' engine, at the end of the accelerator.

When we pick up the Porsche story in the 1975 model year, the company's fortunes were at a low ebb. Total production, entirely of six-cylinder models, totalled 8,640 units, well below the break-even point though a tiny profit was made as a result of Weissach sales, and spare parts turnover. The range con-sisted of the 911 in coupé and Targa forms: the 2.7-litre 911 developed 150 bhp, the 911S developed 175 bhp (or 165 with emission equipment, for the States), and the lusty Carrera 2.7, still with mechanical fuel injection, developed 210 bhp. Heading the range was the new Turbo (type 930), with a 3-litre turbo-charged engine producing 260 bhp.

Fortunes improved considerably in the 1976 model year when 12,000 cars were made at Zuffenhausen and more than 8,000 early 924s went down the line

Above *The 911 made its debut at Frankfurt in September 1963, although it was then known as the 901. It went into production a year later, and has remained popular for nearly a quarter of a century.*

Below *The VW-Porsche 914 remained in production until 1975, although six-cylinder versions were discontinued in 1971.*

Porsche had two six-cylinder engine sizes in the mid-1970s, the 2.7-litre powering the 'cooking' model and the 3-litre, 200 bhp version for the Carrera. The Targa version illustrated is a Carrera, with wider wheel arches than the 911.

at Neckarsulm. Of the 12,000, 7,313 were 911s, 1,531 were Carreras and 1,157 were Turbos, a figure that far exceeded predictions; there were also 2,022 type 912s built especially for the American market, replacing the 914 model temporarily.

The Carrera models were not the racy 2.7-litre models beloved by collectors, but had 3-litre engines based on the Turbo's, though of course without the turbo-charger. The magnesium crankcase was substituted by die-cast aluminium, a little heavier but more rigid, and space was allowed for a bore dimension of 3¾ in (95 mm), even 3⅞ in (97 mm) later on; the stroke remained at 27.5 in (70.4 mm) giving a capacity of 2,994 cc for both the Carrera 3 and the Turbo. Bosch K-Jetronic injection replaced the dirty mechanical injection and the power output dropped slightly, to 200 bhp in a model weighing 2,468 lb (1,120 kg). Performance was good, the Carrera 3 able to accelerate to 60 mph (94 km/h) in 6 seconds, to 100 mph (160 km/h) in 15.2 seconds and reach a top speed of 145 mph (232 km/h), all on two-star fuel, but the purists made it clear that they did not approve any reduction in performance, for whatever reason.

Refinements on the 3-litre models included a new, automatically-controlled heating system. A small dial between the seats had markings from 1 to 10 and once the driver had selected the temperature two sensors inside the cabin kept it constant; two levers between the seats were replaced by one, with a red knob, which was automatically controlled (but most people unfamiliar with the car moved the lever manually, immediately breaking the linkage!). Tempostat, a constant speed control, was another innovation, and a year later the 3-litre models were made more luxurious with deep pile carpet, and turn-wheel door locks which increased security.

The 911S was taken out of the range, replaced by the Carrera 3, and this was the root of dissatisfaction among the sporty customers. The S, and the RS, commanded a special affection on account of their urgent response and hard-edged noise, and ownership had a special cachet. The Carrera 3, though with excellent performance and even more torque than the S, was regarded as a soft option, and Professor Bott has referred to the lesson learned: never succeed one popular model with another having less power.

Another soft option, no doubt, was the installation of a brake servo in the 1978 model year cars. It was a good system, reducing pedal effort (especially when the brakes were cold) without spoiling the rock-hard feel of the pedal, and really the only drawback was some loss of luggage space in the front compartment/ All the time the 911 was, in fact, being given wider appeal, exploring

The 911's fascia, little changed in the life of the model, is characteristic. This is a 1976 model, though in recent years smaller sterring wheels have tended to obscure the vital gauges.

the outer boundaries of the sports car market and reaching out to successful, middle-aged business people, entrepreneurs as Peter Schutz says, who could use a 911 on a daily basis and justify its ownership.

In the summer of 1977 (for the 1978 model year) the whole 911 range was realigned as the 928 became available. The Turbo model was introduced with 3.3-litre capacity, and 300 bhp, the Carrera name was rested, and the 911 SC became the standard-bearer of the 'popular' range. It now had the full 3-litre engine rated at 180 bhp (almost midway between the 2.7's 165 and the Carrera 3's 200 bhp), and most of the luxury features installed in the Carrera's bodyshell. The most marked difference was the flare of the wheel arches, to accommodate 6J/7J wheels and 7J/8J wheels were available at extra cost.

There were great celebrations at Zuffenhausen in June 1977 when the 250,000th Porsche was produced. It was a 2.7-litre 911, exported to America, and in 13 years of production the number of six-cylinder models produced was around 170,000, an interesting figure since in 14 years of production the four-cylinder 356 model finally reached a total of 76,000.

In 1979 the ignition timing was 'optimized' and power went up to 188 bhp, and a year later the fundamental decision was made to increase the compression ratio from 8.6:1 to 9.8:1, which with further optimization raised the power output to 204 bhp. Nine years before, the company had chosen to produce the six-cylinder engines with low compression ratios so that they could run on low grades of fuel, down to 92 octane. It had meant that they were less powerful, and less economical than they need be, and with the higher compression came the need to choose 97 octane fuel. Performance was appreciably better, though, with the 911 SC's top speed rising to 146 mph (234 km/h), and fuel economy improved by a surprising 21 per cent overall.

Development of the 911 model was accelerated when Peter Schutz took office at the beginning of 1981, and in September the 911 'Studie' previewed the Cabriolet version which was announced at Geneva six months later. By now the 200,000th 911 had been made, and the Cabriolet was a model that could have been introduced at any time after the Targa was introduced in 1967! Bodily it was virtually a Targa with the roll-over hoop removed, and a very taut soft-top hood design was introduced, with a zip-in plastic window at the back.

As an interesting aside on the Cabriolet, Professor Bott had actually made such a car in the summer of 1980, and it was sometimes to be seen on the test track. No doubt it was developed with a nod and a wink from Professor Porsche but no-one, not even Bott, dared tell Professor Fuhrmann of its existence! It only became official in January 1981, the first month of Peter Schutz's appointment, and was to form one of the main features of the 'Studie' at Frankfurt nine months later.

The Sport version was very appealing, now featuring a Turbo-style 'tea tray' rear spoiler, and Turbo-type Fuchs wheels with black centres and polished alloy rims, uprated shock absorbers and sport seats. In the 1983 model year, 4,277 Cabriolets were made and 2,752 Targas, but a year later the figures were reversed as 3,793 Targas surpassed the 3,103 Cabriolets, though the totals were very similar. By now a new primary silencer had been introduced to reduce noise and emissions, and the heating/ventilation system had been improved again, finally deleting the confusing red lever between the seats.

If anyone still felt that the 911 model had gone soft, the response came in August 1983 with the announcement of the Carrera 3.2. With 231 bhp available, this was the most powerful and quickest normally-aspirated production-line model ever offered to the public, capable of reaching 60 mph (96 km/h) from rest in 5.3 seconds, 100 mph (160 km/h) in 13.6 seconds and a maximum speed of 152 mph (243 km/h).

The use of the Carrera name was justified, for although in former days it was used only to denote a model intended for racing, in this day and age competitions cars are ever more specialized (956 Carrera, or 962 Carrera, just does not sound right somehow), and the connotation of the name put customers in the right frame of mind.

The Carrera retained the 3¾ in (95 mm) bore but adopted the Turbo's crank-shaft and connecting rods, the stroke being increased to 3 in (74.4 mm) and the capacity to 3,164 cc. It was said that 80 per cent of the engine was new; domed pistons raised the compression ratio from 9.8 to 10.3:1, and a new flywheel was needed to serve the Bosch Digital Motor Electronics (DME) ignition systm, a far more sophisticated method of adjusting the ignition 'map' according to engine load, speed, temperatures, even battery voltage. The box of electronics was placed under the driver's seat, for the 911 was now crammed with equipment, switches and gadgets that Butzi Porsche never knew about when he designed the model.

Within the engine, the age-old problem of timing chain tensioner failures was finally eliminated, after at least a dozen attempts, with a new type served by the engine's dry-sump oil system. The new tensioner could be retro-fitted, removing one anxiety from the purchase of a used car.

Improvements went right through the 911 Carrera. The brakes, for example, were better for being ⅛ in (3.5 mm) thicker, assisted by a larger 8 in (204 mm) servo from the Turbo model, and the 928's rear brake pressure limiting device was adopted to improve stability in emergency stops.

In the transmission, fourth and fifth gears were raised to suit the extra per-formance, and an external oil cooler was fitted to the gearbox. Now the Carrera accelerated in fourth gear like the 3-litre model did in third, and in fifth like the 3-litre did in fourth, and as an extra bonus there was no penalty in fuel consumption (though neither was there any improvement, for a change). Among the refinements inside the Carrera, the heating system was revised again adopting the Turbo's twin-fan control for the footwells; the sunroof option featured a better wind deflector, and the Targa model was given better weather sealing. Visually, the Carrera received the 'telephone dial' cast alloy wheels, with the popular Fuchs spoke-style wheels (first introduced on the 911S in 1966) as an option.

A further option, and an expensive one, was the M-491 'Turbo-look' body kit for all versions, coupé, Targa and Cabriolet. This had the substantially-flared

wheel arches allowing the use of much wider wheels, 8J and 9J in section, the Turbo's rear wheel spacers, brakes and suspension. It did not appeal to everyone, of course, since the greater frontal area actually slowed the Carrera down, to below 150 mph (240 km/h) in absolute terms; but to those who buy their Porsches on visual appeal, there was even a detachable aluminium hardtop made for the Cabriolet, costing DM10,000 and another option for the soft-top was an electrically-operated hood control.

A redesigned fascia panel introduced for the 1986 model year incorporated larger fresh air ducts, and automatic temperature control was improved by moving the main sensor from above the windscreen to the top of the dashboard. New front seats were standardized and these were mounted ¾ in (20 mm) lower, with a greater range of adjustment. Central door locking became a feature, using the latest infra-ray technique for remote control.

Underneath, the suspension system was generally uprated with thicker anti-roll bars and rear torsion bars, and new settings for the gas dampers, aimed at improving the handling without spoiling the ride comfort.

For 1987 (and no further changes are expected for 1988) a new gearshift pattern was introduced, taking reverse gear away to the left and up, instead of to the right, and the diameter of the lever was reduced. Of greater importance, perhaps, the power of the catalyzed model was improved quite substantially; emission controlled Carreras had been available since the end of 1984 with 207 bhp, but this figure was increased to 217 bhp. Finally, the clutch was given

The 911 range came back with a new lease of life in 1983 when the 3.2-litre Carrera model was announced in Coupé, Cabriolet and Targa forms (the Coupé is illustrated with optional Sport equipment including wide wheels and rear wing). The 231 bhp engine, the standard model in fact, gave a performance very close to that of the original 3-litre Turbo model to which many enthusiasts aspired.

hydraulic control, rather a belated improvement, making it lighter in operation.

One thing that was welcome was the incorporation of twin rear foglamps in the red reflector strip across the tail. Previously one red lamp had been hung, rather untidily, underneath the bumper where it was damage-prone, and it is surprising what a big difference such a small tidying-up measure can make to the car's appearance. In addition, the front tyres were increased in section, from 185/70 to 195/65, with VR ratings of course, and the headlamp beam could be adjusted from the driving seat, as in the 928.

Had the 911 model been left alone for years at a time, as other manufacturers would tend to do, it could never have retained its evergreen appeal, remaining the world's most desirable sports car even as it nears its 25th anniversary. It is ironic, too, that in 1984, the year that was destined for its demise, more than 14,000 911s were built, not far from the best-ever figures for a year, and demand continues at similar high levels.

Such was the publicity attached to the 959, and the fact that it incorporates a lot of new technology for the 911 model, that Porsche had to issue a statement early in 1987 denying that any major changes were intended for the six-cylinder in the 1988 model year. By now the 250,000th 911 had been made, and the 300,000 mark will be in sight at the end of the decade.

911 Turbo—A winner!

When the 911 Turbo (type 930) was announced at the Paris Show in October 1974 there was a need to build at least 400 examples to gain Group 4 homologation, and to form a basis for the 934 and 935 racing cars. Nine years later the total produced passed the 10,000 mark, and was well on the way towards the 15,000th edition, as the Turbo was reintroduced to the American market after an absence of six years.

Some saw the Turbo as an evolution of the 911 Carrera RSR 3.0, plus a turbocharger. That was a fairly exotic racing model based on the road model, and a total of 109 were built. Dr Fuhrmann could not see how four times that number of Turbos could be made, unless they were given a completely fresh appeal. His order went out, that the Turbo was not an 'evolution' at all, but would be a luxurious, no-expense-spared supercar to rival the best models in Ferrari's range. The competitions cars would be evolved from the 930, not the other way round.

All the basic development work had been carried out in the 1974 racing season by Ing Norbert Singer, a KKK turbo-charger being applied to a 2.1-litre flat-six to produce 520 bhp. The flared bodywork and the running gear was incorporated in the RSR, and it was that version's 3-litre engine that would form the basis for the 930's power unit. As told, the 911 Carrera Turbo finished second at Le Mans despite facing many smaller, lighter and equally powerful sports-prototypes, and pressure was taken off the programme when FISA postponed the advent of the new formula until 1976. That, at least, gave Porsche plenty of time to homologate the Turbo and develop the 935 and 936 racing cars.

Above The 'prototype' 911 Turbo was raced in 1974, seen here at Le Mans where it finished second overall. The rear arches and massive wing were almost grotesque, but the 2.1-litre turbo was surprisingly fast.

Right The first turbo, run by Dr Fuhrmann in 1974, had the 3-litre engine installed in a Carrera bodyshell, and it was actually faster in a straight line than the production model which had wider wheel arches.

In their first year the Turbos were equipped with Pirelli Cinturato tyres on 15-inch diameter Fuchs forged alloy wheels.

The Turbo went into production early in 1975 and had few peers on the road. The turbo-charged engine developed 260 bhp, but the 911's five-speed gearbox (type 915) was thought to be inadequate for 254 lbft (35.3 mkg) of torque (at 4,000 rpm) so the Turbo had a new transmission with only four forward gears, with wider teeth, inside the casing.

In standard form the Turbo had air conditioning, electrically-operated windows, leather upholstery and other luxury features, and at DM67,850 it was nearly twice the price of the 911 2.7. The bodywork was special in having massive flares on the wheel arches, to accommodate 7J and 8J rims, the wheels themselves being the Fuchs style forged alloy type. The flares were, however, introduced for homologation reasons, the rear wheels needing spacers to fill the arches, and Dr Fuhrmann personally ran a narrower Carrera with the Turbo's running gear. . . it was faster!

The suspension system relied more upon series production models than was

The Turbo model has changed little since 1978 and is due for major revisions. It offers massive performance with complete docility, and production remains higher than ever expected.

Above *Established in Porsche's line-up in 1966, the 911 Targa has remained very popular. The fixed glass rear window allows the car to be as snug as a coupé in the winter.*

Below *The 959 is the ultimate version of the 911 model, having a 450 bhp engine, six-speed transmission and four-wheel drive among its many attributes. All three main ranges (4, 6 and 8 cylinder) will benefit from the new technology.*

expected, retaining torsion bar springing at the back though with larger dimension cast aluminium trailing arms and bigger bearings, while at the front the MacPherson struts were angled to produce anti-dive characteristics. The brakes were massive, 12 in (30 cm) in diameter and fully ventilated, though cross-drilling was stopped because there was insufficient experience of this technique for a production model.

With a bore and stroke of 3⅜ × 2⅞ in (95 × 70.4 mm) the Turbo's capacity was 2,994 cc, and the engine ran with a 6.5:1 compression ratio. The turbo-charging technique was still quite new in road cars, though BMW had pioneered it in the late 1960s for a racing version of the 2002 and Porsche had accumulated vast experience in Can-Am competitions. The turbo-charger waste-gate was set to allow a pressure of 0.7 bar (10 lb) of boost, and power was delivered in copious quantities from 3,000 rpm onwards. It was, though, not the easiest of cars to take off the line quickly since the engine sometimes 'bogged down', spinning the plates in the larger 9.5 in (240 mm) clutch. Initial acceleration tended to be a little slower than the 3-litre Carrera's but once under way the Turbo would gain handsomely, reaching 100 mph (160 km/h) in under 13 seconds.

The big front air dam, and the large spoiler on the lid of the engine com-partment, provided sufficient downforce for 150 mph (240 km/h) performance, the 'tray' reducing lift from nearly 400 lb (180 kg) to just 38 lb (17 kg). The Turbo was not just a very fast car, though. The turbo-charger muted the exhaust noise and the flat-six never had the glorious sound of a Ferrari boxer, but the Porsche was completely tractable in urban traffic, and was quickly recognized as a thoroughly practical model for everyday use. It had a six-year anti-corrosion

For the 1976 model year Pirelli's new P7 tyres became standard equipment for the Turbo, and 16-inch diameter rims were an option (they were standardized a year later).

In 1978 the Turbo model reached a form that would last for 10 years, at 3.3-litres and 300 horsepower. The addition of an intercooler dictated a new type of rear spoiler, and 917 type racing brakes were fitted as standard equipment.

warranty from the start, as well as the usual 12-month unlimited mileage mechanical warranty.

Six months into the production run the Turbo became equipped, as standard, with Pirelli's new P7 tyres, 205/50 VR 15 at the front and 225/50 at the rear. Porsche had helped the Italian company develop these tyres for ultra-rapid road cars, making the huge peripheral drum at Weissach available to them. Roadholding performance was certainly improved, but now it became even more difficult to slingshot the Turbo off the line, such was the grip.

A by-pass valve was built into the turbo's wastegate system, preventing sudden build-up of pressure and giving the engine altogether better characteristics. Although the boost pressure was raised to a maximum of 0.8 bar (11 lb) the power came in more gradually, from 2,500 rpm. Another improvement was the adoption of an electrically operated, and heated, rear-view mirror.

A very popular colour combination was white, with Martini stripes tastefully adorning the flanks. A special show car was built for the British motor show in 1976 and it was immediately dubbed the 'Martini Turbo', and overnight everyone wanted one just like that! The extremely expensive seats were made up of blocks of leather-covered foam material, the 'Dr Fuhrmann seats' as they were called, being finished with alternate blue, red and white panels. Martini, the Italian vermouth company, had successfully sponsored Porsche to a pair of World Championships on the circuits in 1976, and the pay-off was tremendous publicity among the Porsche fraternity, and beyond it.

Sixteen-inch diameter wheel rims were standardized for the 1977 model year, allowing a better circulation of air around the brakes, and there were numerous detail changes including twin fuel pumps of a new design, a boost gauge incorporated in the rev-counter dial, an over-centre auxiliary spring on the clutch pedal, a brake servo for left-hand drive markets, improved synchromesh in the gearbox, a new type of front anti-roll bar, new rear trailing arms with easier ride-height adjustment, a centre console which stored cassette tapes and carried the air conditioner controls, a rear window wiper and two-stage rear window demisting.

The 911 Turbo moved into its next definitive form (largely unchanged in the next decade) when the engine's bore was increased to 3¾ in (97 mm), and the capacity went up to 3,299 cc. An air-to-air intercooler was inserted into the space above the engine, dictating a new 'tea-tray' type of spoiler, and the disc brakes were now cross-drilled for better cooling, and gripped by four-piston callipers identical to those on the former type 917 racing cars.

In terms of performance the Turbo was now firmly ahead in the supercar league, with a top speed of 160 mph (256 km/h). *Motor* rated it as the world's fastest accelerating road car, able to reach 60 mph (96 km/h) from rest in 5.3 seconds, 100 mph (160 km/h) in 12.3 seconds and 120 mph (192 km/h) in 19.1 seconds, all with an average fuel consumption of 15.9 mpg (17.5 litres/100 km).

The power was increased to 300 bhp (at 5,500 rpm), the torque by 20 per cent from 254 to 303 lbft (35 to 42 mkg) at 4,000 rpm, a higher compression ratio of 7:1 making its contribution. There were many new features in the engine,

Left *An increase in bore, to 97 mm, was enough to raise the Turbo's engine capacity to 3,299 cc (1979 model year). The air-to-air inter-cooler, served by the new type of spoiler, found a home above the cooling fan.*

Right *The Porsche 'Studie' at Frankfurt in September 1971 was a mixture of things to come. First the Cabriolet top, announced for the 911 (but not the Turbo) in 1982; then four-wheel drive, for the 959 model; and finally the Turbo Cabriolet, shown definitively at Frankfurt in 1987!*

though, since it had a new crankshaft, and larger main and connecting rod bearings. The transmission was improved with a new type of clutch-disc hub, more flexible than the previous design and eliminating the gear teeth chatter which had been a characteristic at idle. The engine had to be moved back 1.18 in (30 mm) in the chassis to accommodate the new clutch, (and the recommended pressures for the rear tyres rose from 34 to 43 psi.)

The Turbo model was withdrawn from the American market from the end of 1979 until 1986, resulting in the production level falling to 1,000 units a year for a while, but there was one more stage of development to come. In 1982 the ignition was given further optimization, a new warm-up regulator and fuel distributor were installed, and a twin tailpipe exhaust system, with reduced back pressure, was specified. Power remained at 300 bhp but the torque figure rose from 303 to 318 lbft (42 to 44 mkg), and the Turbo proved measurably quicker. *Autocar* found the top speed to be 162 mph (259 km/h), and recorded 5.1 seconds to 60 mph (96 km/h) and 12.2 seconds to 100 mph (160 km/h). Then, in a specially-staged event in Britain John Morrison established a time of 23.985 seconds for the standing kilometre, leaving behind a Lamborghini Countach, an

Aston Martin Vantage and a Lotus Esprit Turbo.

Central locking and electrically-adjustable seats followed in 1984, when the anti-roll bars were increased in diameter by ⅛ in (2 mm) to ⅞ in (22 mm) front and ¾ in (20 mm) rear, and a larger brake servo was fitted to reduce the pedal pressure by 30 per cent. A year later new and lower seats were fitted in order to increase comfort and headroom, and the rear wheel rims were increased to 9 in (228 mm) section, carrying 245/45 VR 16 tyres. In 1986 the Turbo shared the Carrera's refinements, including the integral rear foglamps.

Although the Porsche factory had denied since 1981 that the Turbo model was suitable for conversion, on account of its power, several private body-shops had carried out neat cabriolet body styles. It was rather surprising therefore that the Porsche factory introduced the 911 Turbo in Targa and cabriolet forms for the 1988 model year, with suitable stiffening in the floorpan. As Peter Schutz would say, it was 'do-able'; it was just curious that it took so long.

It was not just the numerous styling shops that attend to Porsches: the factory has its own, based in the Customer Department at Works 1, where Rolf Sprenger is in charge of converting any Porsche model to the whim of the customer. Since 1981 the factory has been able to offer a 'Flachbau' (flat profile) 911/Turbo nose, along the lines of the 935's, and in 1983 a very special Turbo was made for Mansour Ojjeh, the Arabian head of the TAG company which was paying for the Porsche-designed Formula 1 engine.

Above and left *While Dr Fuhrmann preferred his Turbo engine in a 'narrow' 911, some customers wanted their 911s to have the Turbo's appearance. Porsche catered for them, introducing the M-481 wide body style in Coupé, Targa and Cabriolet forms.*

Above right and right *The 'Flachbau' (flat-front) version of the 911 and Turbo proved so popular with specialist builders that Porsche set up its own production line, producing some 250 each year. Most were reserved for the American market. Added to the 911 range in 1988 is the Speedster version, with a lowered, detachable windscreen.*

Ojjeh ordered a cross between a 934 and a 935 racing car, complete with a huge rear wing, and with fully-retracting headlamps similar to those of the 924. The interior was opulent—this was the first Porsche ever to feature a walnut dashboard, as well as leather upholstery—and power was kept down to 380 bhp in the interest of easy driving. The top speed was not disclosed, but was certainly over 190 mph (304 km/h).

Once this project had been publicized in Porsche's superb journal, *Christophorus*, a trickle of customers became a flood. Numerous German and American bodyshops such as Rinspeed, Koenig, Gemballa, Strosek, b+b, and Pristine Porsche jumped on the bandwagon, to such effect that the Porsche company itself had to take the matter seriously.

Sprenger's customer department could make two Flachbau models every three weeks, but in 1986 the version was incorporated into the company's production capability, with a special line being prepared at the adjacent Rösslebau factory, alongside the area where the 959s were built. By the end of 1986 Porsche had the capability to build one flat-front 911 every day, say 250 in a year, of which 200 would be exported to America, leaving only 50 for Germany and the rest

Left *Even in 1981, Porsche's artist took the 'Studie' concept a stage further with drawings of the Turbo Cabriolet and Targa... while the management continued to insist that the 300 bhp model would be weakened!*

Above right *At Frankfurt in September 1987 Porsche finally unveiled the models that wealthy customers awaited, the Turbo coupé and Targa.*

of the world! In 1988 production of the Flachbau, and of the 911 Turbo Cabriolet, will be fully integrated into the new 911 production line in Works 5, possibly preparing the way for a flat-front 911 as a standard model. It has passed the American and European safety tests and, if the design became standard it will be one of the world's most anticipated announcements. . . though of course, there will always be those who think a proper 911 has traditional lights that can always be seen.

Porsche Cars Great Britain, for one, introduced the Flachbau as a special version, available to order. As well as the aerodynamic frontal treatment the '911 Turbo with Sport Equipment' had its power raised to 330 bhp with higher profile camshafts, larger turbo-charger and intercooler, and a modified exhaust system. The car was said to accelerate to 62 mph (100 km/h) in 5.2 seconds and to have a maximum speed of 171 mph (274 km/h).

Such luxury has its price, of course. In Britain the conversion raised the Turbo's value by 88 per cent, and after the inevitable price increases of 1986, that meant that the Turbo cost £50,000 and the Sport version £90,000. That, however, purchased the fastest and rarest Porsche on the road, an asset that a few people are always willing and able to acquire.

911s in competition

The result of the ADAC 1,000-Kilometres of the Nürburgring in 1970 was by no means untypical of the era: 15 Porsches were in the top 20 places in the classification, and behind the factory 908s and the Ferraris was a wall-to-wall covering of older 906s, 911s and even a couple of 914/6s. In reply to those who

Three racing models appeared in 1976, all developed from the 1974 racing programme, and they were totally successful. The 934 (pictured at the Nürburgring Karussel) won the European Grand Touring Car Championship, the 935 won the World Championship for Manufacturers, and the 936, pictured at Le Mans, won the 24-Hour race, and the World Sports Car Championship. In common, their six-cylinder turbo-charged engines were based on the 911's.

complained about 'bloody Porsches, dominating everything,' I begged to question, in *Motoring News*, how the competition would look *without* Porsche!

The Stuttgart firm has been the backbone of endurance racing for three decades, and while the factory team always chose to enter the fastest, purpose-built machines that the regulations allowed, its customers were just as successful, with the 356 and then with the 911, in the Grand Touring categories, and without them many competitions would have been far poorer.

The 911 Carrera RS programme of 1973/74, with engines of 2.7 to 3-litre capacity, was the last major development of the normally-aspirated engine for competitions. The Carrera RS won both the Daytona 24-Hour race and the Targa Florio in 1973, historic successes which conclusively marked the 911 as an all-time classic, but in 1974 the factory moved on to the turbo-charged development, the 911 Carrera Turbo, managed by Norbert Singer. Customers, notably Erwin Kremer and Georg Loos but including many leading privateers, mopped up just about every race, cup and championship available in Europe, while in America Peter Gregg was the foremost entrant and driver. BMW and Ford vied strongly in touring car championship racing while Porsche ruled the roost in GT, apart from minor incursions from de Tomaso, Alpine-Renault and privateer Ferraris, none of which made any memorable impression.

While turbo-charging development seemed suitable for circuit racing, there was still a career for the 911 in rallies despite the arrival of a new breed of lightweight, purpose-built cars such as the Alpine-Renault and the Lancia Stratos. The East African Safari Rally was one that Porsche had tried to conquer

without success, and in 1974 Bjorn Waldegaard made another attempt, almost successful, in a standard engined RS 2.7. He was leading the event by miles until a driveshaft broke during the last night, and the Swede had to settle for second place.

The Porsche factory hardly noticed an entry for Jean-Pierre Nicolas by the Almeras brothers in the 1978 Monte Carlo Rally, but 'Jumbo' had the drive of his life in a snow-bound event, coming through to vanquish the Lancia and Renault factory teams which suffered from a poor choice of tyres.

Plans had already been laid to tackle the Safari once again, and the Monte success was a real encouragement. Martini sponsorship was arranged for two 911s, which appeared with a glaring yet attractive colour scheme—there was no chance of missing them on a dark night! Waldegaard again drove the lead car, backed by Vic Preston Junior. Now, though, the event was faster than ever and the Porsches suffered a number of failures with the rear shock absorbers. Preston, who had never rallied in a Porsche before, managed to gain second place while Waldegaard, who had endured worse difficulties, climbed up from thirteenth place to fourth at the end.

Privately-entered 911s continued to do well in tarmac rallies, Bernard Beguin for instance winning the 1979 Tour d'Ypres, but for the time being the factory's attention was focused on four-cylinder development. Under Schutz's management, though, with anything do-able, there was a re-awakening of

Left *The year 1978 started well for Porsche; while Dr Fuhrmann was in Monte Carlo for the Car of the Year presentation, Jean-Pierre Nicolas reached the Principality as winner of the Monte Carlo Rally, totally unexpected for the 911.*

Above right *Following the Monte victory, Porsche tried once more to win the East African Safari. The Martini sponsored cars finished second and fourth.*

Right *The ultimate Porsche factory 935 was 'Moby Dick', the 935/78 with water-cooled cylinder heads and 750 hp. It won the Silverstone 6-Hours but was dropped down the order by a misfiring engine at Le Mans.*

Top *Porsche built a series of 20 911 SC RS models in 1983, the weight down to 960 kg and the power up to 255 bhp. Henri Toivonen, driving the Rothmans entry, was second overall in the European Rally Championship.*

Above *The racing 962 model was introduced to the American IMSA series in January 1984, when Mario and Michael Andretti drove the works car at Daytona. Powered by a single-turbo, air-cooled engine as the regulations demanded, the engine was very similar to that of the 1976 935 model, and not so far removed from the road-going Turbo.*

interest in 1983 when circuit sponsors Rothmans enquired at top level whether Porsche would co-operate with their rally programme. There was an element at Weissach, led by Juergen Barth, that never lost an opportunity to promote the cause of rallying, and a 911 had been found for reigning World Rally Champion Walter Rohrl in 1981, for an entry in the Manx Rally.

Rothmans had not enjoyed a good rally season in 1983, with outdated Opels, and Porsche went to the trouble of building 20 911 SC RS models in order to secure evolution homologation for what must be the most exciting non-turbo six-cylinder version ever seen.

The series of 20 cars was built down to 2,112 lb (960 kg), while the 3-litre engine was taken up to 255 bhp. All the usual tricks were used to reduce the weight, including the use of GFK aluminium for the front and rear bumpers, the front and rear lids and the doors; Glaverbel lightweight glass saved a few kilos, as did the fitting of lightweight seats and the elimination of all the sound-proofing. Putting some weight back, though, the suspension was uprated with auxiliary springs, and cross-drilled Turbo ventilated disc brakes were installed.

Even this, however, was not enough to keep track of the four-wheel drive, turbo-charged Audis, and raising the engine power to 290 bhp barely kept Rothmans' lead driver Henri Toivonen in touch. Toivonen, son of former Porsche exponent Pauli, won the Ypres 24-Hours, the Milles Pistes, the Costa Smeralda and Madeira rallies and was runner-up in the European Rally Championship, despite missing some events with a back injury.

In the Middle East Championship Saeed Al Hajri, from Qatar, and John Spiller enjoyed a great deal of success for Rothmans, winning the series in dominant style. At the end of the season, Rothmans entered two cars in the RAC Rally of Great Britain, one for Roger Clark who finished eleventh and another for Al Hajri who finished seventeenth. Both cars had run well, but been heavily outclassed by the Audis, Peugeots and Lancias.

There was now no point in continuing without four-wheel drive and a turbo-charger, and the factory was busy preparing the 959 model which won the Paris-Dakar 'Raid' in Janury 1984; more of that in the next chapter. Doubts were increasing about that programme as well, in the strict competitive sense, for in 1985 even Audi was overshadowed by the Peugeot and Lancia 'forest racers' and

The Porsche 935 specially developed by the Kremer brothers won the Le Mans 24-Hours in 1979, after the prototypes had fallen by the wayside.

it was becoming increasingly evident that in Group B nothing less than a purpose-built car would stand a chance of winning anything.

The 934 and 935 programmes were totally successful and their record does not need repeating, except to summarize that the 935 became the most successful competitions car ever to wear the Porsche crest. In eight seasons the 935 won 42 World Championship events and some 70 IMSA championship races in America, while the 956 and 962 Group C/IMSA successors continued the winning streak from 1982/83 onwards. . . still, basically, with the same production-derived engine.

Of all the 935's successes, the most outstanding must be victory at Le Mans in 1979, when the car entered by Kremer Porsche Racing defeated the opposition, and the elements in the hands of Klaus Ludwig, and Don and Bill Whittington. Not far behind was another 935 driven by Rolf Stommelen, Dick Barbour and film star Paul Newman. All the prototypes had run into trouble during the race, Porsche losing its pair of Essex Petroleum liveried 936s (one with a tyre failure which damaged the cooling system, the other with an alternator failure out of reach of the pits).

For the first time in many years the French classic race was won by a production-based car, and that was significant. Ever since the war, the race had been won by a car prepared specially for the race, though a number of them concurrently had production equivalents, or production successors. Wild as the 935 was in terms of race preparation, it was undoubtedly the derivation of a popular production car, and its success is not likely to be repeated until such time as FISA, or the Automobile Club de l'Ouest, changes the rules to favour such machines.

The Turbo based 935 was still a highly effective race car in 1982, when John Fitzpatrick and David Hobbs finished fourth at Le Mans — behind a trio of new 956s.

6

A crystal ball: the 959

Never has a new model been more keenly anticipated than the Porsche 959, and that statement applies particularly to the 200 customers who placed DM50,000 deposits on the full price of DM420,000 in 1985, and had to wait for two or three years to take delivery of their ultimate supercar.

Today, the parts of the 959 are as much of interest as the whole, for this is the prototype vehicle synthesizing components which will find their way into full production in the next decade, and not only in the 911 range. The engine, with four valves per cylinder and water-cooling for the heads, is similar to that in the 962 racing car, though not identical; the transmission is a six-speed gearbox, surely not developed merely for 200 cars; the four-wheel drive system is a masterpiece in electronic engineering (cleverer possibly than the people who will use it!), self-levelling, fully-adjustable suspension is something that is likely to be adopted for the eight cylinder cars as well, in time, and a new turbo-charging technique is used, twin KKK units working in tandem to provide a near-stepless power increment.

As Professor Porsche has said, a four-wheel drive version of the 911 was near readiness in 1975, so the appearance of the 'Studie' at Frankfurt in September 1981 was well planned. The Turbo's cabriolet style, which preceded the 911 Cabriolet model by 18 months, had been prepared by Professor Bott in 1980, but what was interesting was the four-wheel drive system, shown by a mirror underneath the car. It was extremely rudimentary; in fact the Studie was not even a runner, but it showed a driveshaft running forward from the gearbox (ahead of the rear engine, as usual) to a 924 Turbo differential between the front wheels, and driveshafts applied to each front wheel with its suspension modified to accept torque.

After the debut, work began immediately on development of the 'Gruppe B' study which appeared two years later, at Frankfurt in 1983. As the name implies it was the forerunner of 200 identical cars which could gain access to FISA's Group B homologation list, and it was fully intended that the model would be as invincible in rallies as the 956 was in racing. Circuit partner Rothmans were deeply interested in the project, and in 1983 the 911 SC RS model was made as a limited series to keep the programme going, until the Group B car was homologated. It was hoped that all 200 cars would be made and sold by the middle of 1985, and that the Rothmans-Porsche team would be fully operational by the end of that season.

Professor Bott, with the support of Peter Schutz, took a leaf from Professor Fuhrmann's book and insisted that this would be no mere homologation vehicle. It must, he said, be attractive to behold, extremely luxurious, and must represent the pinnacle of technical achievement. With so many new and rare features in the specification it could hardly be anything else, in fact, and unless well equipped it could not possibly appeal to extremely wealthy customers—all 200 of them.

Events overtook the Group B plan, however. When conceived, the Audi Quattro was the king of rallying, a relatively heavy production-based coupé with a turbo-charged 2.2-litre engine. The Group B Porsche might have beaten that in time (although, with its engine overslung at the rear, some doubted even that). Rather, it was the emergence of the purpose-built Peugeot 205 Turbo 16 forest-racer in 1984 that set all the alarm bells ringing, for here was a mid-engined racing car, incredibly small and nimble, down to 2,200 lb (1,000 kg) with plenty of turbo-charged horsepower available to the driver. Lancia, Ford and Austin announced plans to build similar machines and the pace-setting Audi was quickly rendered obsolete.

Below *The 'Gruppe B' study appeared at the Frankfurt Show in September 1983, and while the windscreen and doors clearly indicated its 911 origin, every other line was transformed. This was the first 4-wd Porsche, but few believed that the svelte lines would survive the Sahara Desert four months later!*

Right *Within two months of the Gruppe B's German debut the lines had changed significantly, as these year-end factory pictures show. The headlamps and turn indicators have been changed, but significantly there are substantial louvres at the corners to cool the brakes (front) and turbo-chargers (rear), and intercooler ducts appear on the leading edges of the rear wings.*

Left *The 1984 Paris-Dakar Raid entries — one of them the winner — were 'conventional' Porsche 911 rally cars in most respects, save the four-wheel drive system. This featured an Audi Quattro differential between the front wheels, directing 30 per cent of the engine's 225 bhp to the front by purely mechanical means.*

Below *Three Porsche 911 four-wheel drive cars were entered in the Paris-Dakar Raid, sponsored by the company's circuit partners Rothmans. René Metge's (176) won the rally outright, Jacky Ickx was sixth and Roland Kussmaul, the 'technical sweeper', was twenty-sixth.*

Right A car that has spent three weeks in the desert, and been rolled, is hard to restore to showroom condition... Porsche didn't even try! Kussmaul's 1984 Raid 911 was driven by the author on its return to Germany, and the four-wheel drive system provided an unusual experience on the MAN proving ground. The engine is a 3-litre normally-aspirated flat-six.

Below The rear seat of the 911 Raid cars was replaced by a supplementary fuel tank increasing the total capacity to 260 litres, the cars having a maximum driving range of 1,440 kilometres. This living room for two, for three weeks, carried a large fire extinuisher, water, medical supplies, a radio transmitter and emergency flares.

On the 1984 Paris-Dakar Raid, the sixth placed entry of Jacky Ickx/Claude Brasseur, which survived a wiring loom burn-out.

Winning the 1984 Paris-Dakar Raid was a notable achievement for the Porsche, though the four-wheel drive system was still rudimentary and it was powered by a normally-aspirated engine. Time was passing by, though, and while it became increasingly unlikely that it would ever become a serious rally car production plans were also faltering. Professor Bott explains it this way: 'The 959 is one-and-a-half years late now, but we have learned a lot. It came at a time when we had so many other priorities, like catalyst engines, here at Weissach and it was difficult to find the right priority for the 959.

'Also the suppliers had problems. Many manufacturers went to Bosch for instance, because they couldn't meet the new emission requirements with carburettors. They needed fuel injection systems, and they wanted them quickly; we were competing with Mercedes and BMW, and a lot more. Our 959 was a small production, we needed just 200 units, and the suppliers were not interested. They gave preference to customers making 300 or 400 cars each day, which I can understand, so we had to wait for two, three or four months at a time for parts from our suppliers.'

Nor was that the only problem. In 1983 Porsche adopted the policy of making 'world market' cars, and all future engines would produce the same power and be equally suitable for markets which required the installation of emission equipment. That in itself required a vast amount of development work on the race-derived engine, the installation of a three-way catalyst system in a very short length of exhaust piping causing enormous problems. The decision taken early in 1986 not to export the 959 to America after all (on the grounds that it would need so many changes to the body that the price would escalate) seemed to have made redundant much of the development work, but Paul Hensler has said that although only three German customers would want the catalyzed version it was necessary to do the work as part of the showcase.

'We have not missed any of our goals,' says Professor Bott. 'We have met all our specifications, and we haven't lost one customer through the delay. On the contrary, we have more enquiries all the time, and now we have two customers for each car that we'll make.'

If the 959 would not be made in 1985, the second target stated by Peter Falk was to make the 200 959s, and 20 'evolution' 961 models, 'by September or October 1986'. That was a clear-cut statement made on the grounds of completing homologation before a new set of regulations, and 'Group S' formula being talked about might come into effect in 1987. Once again events overtook Porsche, however, and midway through 1986, and six months before the first 959 even went into the assembly stage, FISA announced a ban on Group B rally cars. This followed a number of serious accidents involving rally spectators, and the fatal accident in Corsica which took the life of Henri Toivonen, in a Lancia.

One by one the sporting objectives crumbled. In January 1986 René Metge scored his second Paris-Dakar Raid success for Porsche, this time in the definitive 959 model lacking only the sophisticated, electronically-controlled shock absorber system. At Le Mans the first 961 racing version made a good debut, finishing seventh after surviving an explosive tyre failure, but in America the IMSA competitors were disappointed in the performance of the 961 GTO, which ran into severe tyre problems on the banking. It became increasingly likely that few customers would be found on either side of the Atlantic for the 15 evolution model 961s that Porsche planned to sell, at least not at the rumoured price of DM650,000 apiece. For that sort of money a customer could buy a 962 and still have a budget to run it well, perhaps to win races outright.

The 961's development continued in 1987 in order to race the model again at Le Mans, though again in the IMSA category. Was it now a car with no home to go to? 'Not really, the 961 is a good car,' says Professor Bott. 'The trouble is that there is no competition in the class, and it cannot compete with the Group C cars which are 600 pounds lighter. All we can do with it now is to develop a four-wheel drive system which might one day be suitable for the Group C car.'

Another on-board development, also tested on the Group C racing cars towards the end of the 1986 season, was the Westinghouse Wabco anti-lock brake system. This was not used on the 962 model in 1987, but the 961 was an ideal test-bed. The Westinghouse system was chosen because in 1984 it was the only one available that would work with a locked differential. The anti-lock system is, like many other things, electronically-controlled and problems arose with the frequency, 'and the intelligence of the computers. 'Only Wabco could meet our goal in a given time,' says Professor Bott. 'At the moment it is more sophisticated than Bosch and other types, but there will be new generations at Bosch which will give similar results.'

The customer 959s went into production at the former Rösslebau factory, next door to Works II, in January 1987. The first was delivered in April and the projected rate was four per week, ensuring that the last would be delivered before the middle of 1988. Production director Professor Dr Rudi Noppen explains that the 959s are not built on a normal flow system, 'but in components, like a ship.' At any time 25 cars would be in the assembly stage, and as one finished car went out, another bare shell would be added to the quota. An enormous sigh of relief will be heard at Zuffenhausen when the last customer takes delivery, for the gestation has been long and expensive. When the price of DM420,000 was established in 1984 it seemed a very great deal of money. The deposits accrued interest paid to the customers' accounts but the DM370,000 balance has been savagely eroded by the strengthening Deutschmark where foreign customers are concerned, and the exercise is not one the marketing department would wish to repeat. A technical tour de force is not always a salesman's dream.

The gross revenue of DM84 million does not, by any means, cover the total cost of the 959's development, and a far greater sum (unquantified by the directors) has been assigned to the Porsche development ledger. Both Peter Schutz and Professor Bott emphasize that such an exercise is not likely to be repeated in the foreseeable future ('It is something that can only be afforded in good times, when the dollar is strong,' says Schutz), but the lessons learned, and the technical knowledge gained, will stand Porsche in good stead until the turn of the century. Before that, there should be more good times in store.

The technical triumph

Underneath the curvaceous aramid skin, the 959 starts life much like any other Porsche. The galvanized steel monocoque is made in the normal way, with the same door and window openings though the floorpan is changed to accommodate the substantially-revised transmission, engine and suspension mountings. Once the monocoque has been constructed it is wheeled away some 440 yd (400 m) across a road to the Rösslebau factory hall where the real work begins, transforming the 911 into a car that will travel the *Autobahnen* faster than many light aircraft flying above.

The Gruppe B car that appeared in Frankfurt, Paris and Birmingham in the autumn of 1983 was an almost definitive 959, though the numbering system was not heard outside Weissach until the turn of the year, by which time all four corners of the bodywork had been perforated with large and not unattractive louvres that admitted air to the brakes, and exhausted hot air from the rear of the car.

Apart from the bonded windscreen, all visual changes were below the level of the glass, fully aerodynamic aramid (Kevlar type) bodywork having been super-imposed upon the 911's monocoque. Across the nose are two pronounced intakes, 944 Turbo style, low down and admitting cold air to the water and oil radiators. The headlamps are behind glass, flush with the bodywork, and the wings are substantially flared to accommodate the 17 in (43 cm) diameter, wide-tyred magnesium wheels. The doors and front lid are made of aluminium, while aramid composites continue the wide look along the sills, then up and over the generous rear arches. Beautifully integrated into the aramid engine cover is a wrap-over rear 'wing', and the overall effect of the restyling is to turn the 20-year-old design

Endurance testing for the 959 was carried out, as usual, in the Arctic circle and in the Sahara, and a full-length skid plate was needed for extreme conditions. Details of the new front suspension system and brakes from the 962 can be seen above, and the shoe-horn installation of the now very bulky engine, with 450 bhp, in the lower picture.

into a shape of the future, even while retaining the 911's familiarity. The body is, overall, 10 in (25 cm) wider than the 911's, and the drag coefficient is reduced markedly to 0.32, an exceptional figure considering that uplift at the 200 mph (320 km/h) maximum has been eliminated.

The definitive 959 had another important alteration in that the ducts for the twin intercoolers were switched from the reverse slopes of the rear arches, where they were found to be ineffective, to the forward position aft of the doorhandles. It will also be noted that the power was originally given as 400 bhp and the weight as 2,453 lb (1,115 kg); it was hoped that 200 examples and 20 evolution cars would be built and homologated by April 1985. By the time the first cars were actually delivered well into 1987 the power was quoted at 450 bhp, or 430 bhp with catalytic equipment, and the weight had risen to 3,190 lb (1,450 kg).

The floorpan, as mentioned, had to be heavily revised to accommodate different engine locations, and, more particularly, new suspension mounts. The MacPherson strut (front) and torsion bar (rear) suspensions were scrapped, and replaced by competitions-style upper and lower wishbones and dual, coil-sprung Bilstein adjustable dampers on all four corners. Brakes were taken from the 962 racing car, heavily ventilated and cross-drilled, with fixed four-piston alloy callipers.

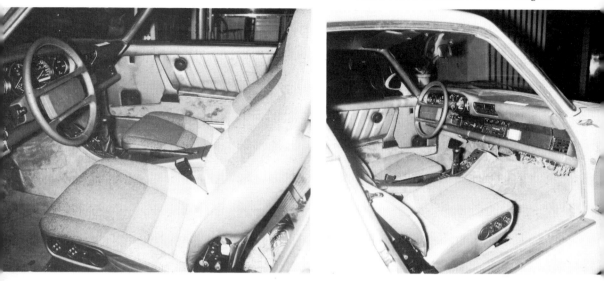

Above *The test mules used in rugged conditions used as much standard equipment as possible, including the electrically-operated seats. The gear lever controls a six-speed transmission.*

Below *Although the 959's aramids clad bodywork is 25 cm wider than that of the 911, the drag coefficient is reduced to 0.32, remarkable for a design with negative uplift at 180 mph.*

Above Porsche's most powerful road car engine, the 450 bhp twin-turbo 959. The cylinder heads are similar to those of the 956/962C racing cars with water cooling, and four valves per cylinder, but the piston barrels remain air cooled. Installed (right) the six-cylinder engine fills the compartment, which has to be adapted.

The Westinghouse Wabco system was preferred to Bosch because it was found to be compatible with the four-wheel drive system, reacting in one-fifth of the time and able, therefore, to sense one wheel locking up in time to influence the clutch-locking mechanism.

Mention should also be made of the wheels and tyres, and their pressure-loss warning system. To meet the very highest safety standards, Dunlop's Denloc tyres were specified, very similar to those supplied to the racing team which have locked beads to keep the tyre safely on the rim even when deflated. They have limited run-flat capability, and many Group C racing drivers have been grateful for their inherent safety. The front tyres are 235/45 section, those at the rear 255/40 section. At a late stage Dunlop failed to homolgate the Denloc for road use, and the 959s were equipped instead with Bridgestore RE71 unidirectional tyres.

As already tested and proven on factory Porsche racing cars since 1980, a pressure-sensing device developed jointly by Robert Bosch and Porsche will light one of four lamps on the fascia should any tyre, or hollow magnesium-spoked wheel, lose pressure. Even at 90 mph (150 km/h) a slow puncture would be dangerous, but at 180 mph (300 km/h) it would be catastrophic.

The twin-turbo-charged power unit, the most powerful ever offered in a road car by any manufacturer, is directly derived from the 956/962 racing engine, though with some important differences. The bore × stroke rtio has been changed a little, from 3⅛ × 2⅞ in (92.8 × 70.4 mm) (2,856 cc) to 3¼ × 2⅜ in (95 × 67 mm) (2,857 cc), and instead of individual, electron-welded cylinder heads, the 959

The dashboard is familiar, but has new features: the torque split control is on the right side of the steering column, hidden from the lens. The display for the chosen torque split is in the right-hand dial, and on the centre console are switches for damper stiffness and ride height.

has one-piece heads for each bank of three cylinders, bolted to the air-cooled block in the normal way, though without gaskets. The heads, with four-valve layout, are water-cooled and have hydraulically-operated inverted cup tappets, unusual in a high-performance engine and remarkable in one that will rev to 8,500 rpm, the normal limit being set at 8,000 rpm. The combustion chambers are similar to those in the racing engines, and the separate cam-box design is retained, but Professor Noppen points out that in the final stages of development the piston bowl was slightly offset and the chain drive to the camshafts modified, significantly reducing the noise output.

Polished titanium connecting rods are fitted, to make the high engine speeds absolutely safe, and with 8.3:1 compression ratio the engine develops 450 bhp at 6,500 rpm, and a maximum of 369 lbft (51 mkg) of torque at 5,500 rpm. There is, though, more than 300 lbft (42 mkg) of torque from 2,200 rpm to 8,000 rpm, ensuring that the 959 is completely docile and driveable in city traffic.

The two KKK turbo-chargers are identical, each having its own intercooler, and they force air to a common plenum chamber on top of the engine. At low engine speeds below 4,000 rpm, the exhaust gases from both banks are directed to the left-hand (primary) turbo-charger and this starts to build up pressure at 1,200 rpm, reaching a maximum of 1 bar (14 lb) at 2,000 rpm. A non-return valve prevents pressure from energizing the right-hand, secondary turbo-charger, which

At very high speeds the Porsche 959 is remarkably stable, and no circumstances, even on the Nürburgring racing circuit, betray the rear-engine layout. Such an achievement is only possible with four-wheel drive, which Porsche has adopted to maximum advantage.

comes into action from 4,000 upwards, to a maximum of 2 bar (28 lb) pressure when the car is driven hard. Turbo response is immediate, therefore, but the engine is extremely tractable.

The installation is completed by a wastegate operated by boost pressure, but controlled by electronics. This limits the boost pressure, and keeps it at the minimum level when the engine is operated at part throttle, thus reducing exhaust back-pressure in the interest of maximum overall engine efficiency. The engine is designed to run on 95 octane unleaded fuel, although for some markets it will also run on 97 octane leaded fuel.

Drive is taken by a racing-type, hydraulically-operated, sintered clutch to a completely new six-speed gearbox, larger than the four- and five-speed transmissions in the 930 and 911, and therefore needing new mounting points. The quoted speeds, at 7,500 rpm, are 37 mph (60 km/h) in first, 64 mph (103 km/h) in second, 93 mph (150 km/h) in third, 127 mph (205 km/h) in fourth, 161 mph (260 km/h) in fifth, and 205 mph (330 km/h) in sixth.

The 959's maximum speed, in fact, is quoted at 'more than 310 km/h' (192 mph), and acceleration times achieved under test at Weissach include 4.3 seconds from rest to 62 mph (100 km/h) and 14.8 seconds to 124 mph (200 km/h), the latter figure being little longer than it takes a 911 Turbo to reach 100 mph (160 km/h).

From the gearbox drive is transmitted to the rear wheels in the normal way, but a supplementary shaft runs forward to what is quite a simple clutch mechanism at the front, with multiple plates, running in oil, and hydraulically clamped but electronically regulated. This offers an almost infinite variety of control, unlike simple (or even complex) mechanical or viscous coupling systems, and this clamping may either be completely controlled by the computer, or partially over-ridden by the driver if, for instance, he anticipates ice ahead. The four lever positions available to the driver are for normal driving on dry roads, for wet surfaces, for snow and ice, and finally a 'traction' mode which locks the clutch for a 50:50 split in emergencies. In effect, they pre-select the drive to the front wheels and determine the amount of understeer that may be experienced, in extreme, and the wise owner will generally leave well alone since the computer can out-perform him in a fraction of the time!

In static state the 959 has a 40:60 weight bias, and under hard acceleration as much as 80 per cent of the weight will transfer to the rear wheels. The limits, therefore, range from 20:80 with the forward clutch plates almost fully apart to 50:50 with them fully clamped, although as a further refinement all the torque could transfer to the front wheels, if the rear wheels were spinning madly on sheet ice. The sophistication of the Porsche system is not only in using electronics to vary the front/rear torque split, but also in programming the computer according to the dynamic weight distribution at each axle, as this relates directly to the load, and the grip available at each tyre. To ease parking, drive to the front wheels is at a minimum at less than 12 mph (20 km/h).

The rolling radius of the front tyres is 1 per cent greater than that of the rear tyres, in order to keep the plates slipping all the time. This increases the efficiency, and improves stability since the front wheels are always 'pulling' the car, rather than the rear wheels 'pushing'. The Westinghouse Wabco brake system, with four channels, was jointly developed by Porsche, and effectively separates the plates in the milli-second that any of the four wheels begins to lock up.

As a further refinement in the transmission, an alternative 'Sport' microchip is available, and fitted to competition cars anyway, offering a more sporting 35:65 torque split as a starting point and generally favouring the rear wheels.

In suspension, the upper and lower control arms for all four wheels are designed to minimize camber change, a normal racing practice, made necessary by the widths of the wheels and tyres. Standard equipment features 8 in (223 mm) front rims and 9 in (229 mm) rear rims, but 10 in (254 mm) rears are available as an option and the 961 competition cars go to the full 12 in (300 mm) widths at the rear, allowed by IMSA regulations. Dual shock absorbers are fitted all round, one of which is electronically adjustable and controlled by speed.

The driver can control three settings which allow ride heights of 120 mm, 150 mm and 180 mm, and the chosen clearance is maintained regardless of the laden weight of the 959. The lowest setting, 120 mm, is the normal one and allows the optimum aerodynamic drag of 0.32, but if the driver selects the medium height setting, of 150 mm, the car will automatically sink to 120 mm at a speed greater than 100 mph (160 km/h) but will not rise again until the speed drops below 93 mph (150 km/h), thus avoiding the suspension 'hunting' at a constant borderline pace. If the 180 mm clearance setting is selected by the driver the car will sink to 150 mm clearance at 50 mph (80 km/h), and to 120 mm at 93 mph (150 km/h).

There are no anti-roll bars as such on the 959, since the hydraulic system interconnecting the shock absorbers does the same job. A small mercury switch detects accelerations in any direction, and effectively pumps up whichever shock absorber is under load. A small electric motor is used to control each of the four 'active' dampers and the maximum reaction time, from one extreme to the other, is half a second.

Another 'first' for the 959, in Porsche's six-cylinder range, is the adoption of power-assisted steering. There is nothing electronic or unusual about the system, but it has been very carefully developed to allow maximum feel to the driver, and was believed necessary because torque reaction at the wide front wheels could make the steering unduly heavy in some circumstances.

The 911's standard ratio of 18.2:1 is retained, but to demonstrate the great care taken to maximize the feedback, the friction has been minimized by specifying a polished, hard-chrome material for the rack, Teflon sealing rings, an outer steel tube for the steering idler shaft, and the universal couplings and bushings are selected and paired; individual parts of the idler rod are assembled by hand to ensure a perfect fit.

In total, the 959 has the highest degree of electronic control yet seen on a car offered for sale. Electronics control every function of the engine, which is not unusual at Porsche, but also the turbo-chargers' wastegate system; electronics control the torque split, the brake system and the shock absorbers. It is no wonder that this is such an expensive machine, and that Professor Bott can claim that 'we have reached optimum reliability in electronic control today.'

_____The 959 and 961 in competition_____

The three cars entered in the 1984 Paris-Dakar Rally were not 959s, in fact, but were described as 911 SC 4-wd Group B prototypes, fairly conventional in having normally-aspirated 3-litre engines tuned, then detuned, to 225 bhp and capable of running on the poorest grades of fuel available in the desert. Where they differed from normal was in having an Audi Quattro differential transmitting 30 per cent of the torque to the front wheels.

Bilstein twin shock absorbers were fitted, adjustable but not electronically-controlled, and the cars weighed 2,717 lb (1,235 kg) without fuel, the tanks in the nose, and in the rear 'passenger seat' areas containing a maximum of 57 gallons (260 litres). Overall the cars used 4 gallons (18 litres) per 62 miles (100 kilometres), allowing a maximum range of 898 miles (1,440 kilometres) though much less in deep sand.

The opposition, extremely varied and including Mercedes G-wagens, Range Rovers, Mitsubishi Pajeros, Renault 4x4s, Lada Nivas and Opel Manta Rallyes, would not be as fast as the Porsches which could run up to 130 mph (210 km/h); what the Porsche team, assembled by Jacky Ickx and sponsored by Rothmans, had to fear was the elements, the chance roll-over or collisions with rocks, and possible frailty in the four-wheel drive system.

In fact Frenchman René Metge, with co-driver Dominique Lemoyne, had a virtually trouble-free run along the 6,820-mile (11,000-kilometre), 20-day course, needing to change only one shock absorber, and the special Dunlop sand tyres did their job perfectly. Metge and Lemoyne won the rally by more than two hours, beating a Range-Rover, a Pajero, an Opel and a Renault, but Jacky Ickx and Claude Brasseur were only sixth after a stone damaged the wiring loom early on, causing a complete electrical burn-out. The third car driven by Weissach technicians Roland Kussmaul and Erich Lerner was twenty-sixth, having been rolled, and then delayed repairing Ickx's car.

I was invited to drive Kussmaul's car soon after it returned to Germany, and had to be impressed by the vivid acceleration, and the way all four wheels scrabbled for grip on the proving ground near Munich. There was an exhilarating sensation of movement as the 911 danced along the tracks, with feedback from the front wheels keeping the steering wheel constantly writhing. Understeer was terminal in slow corners, and the drivers had countered this by throwing the car sideways, on the brakes, when approaching hairpin bends, then flooring the throttle before the apex to swing the tail around. Would a normal rear-drive 911 have been as suitable? Kussmaul dismissed this out of hand: 'When we were practising for the rally a driveshaft broke, and we used up a set of tyres in one day. The car was sideways all the time, and it felt like an old car. Normally we could practise for eight days on a set of tyres, and even on the rally we only changed them every four days.'

The suspension system, standing the floor 11 in (28 cm) off the ground, was unbelievable, with a maximum of 10 in (25 cm) of compression and 3 in (7.5 cm) of rebound. Confronted by a ditch, maybe 12 in (30 cm) deep and 3 ft (90 cm) across, at 70 mph (112 km/h), anyone unfamiliar with the machine would brace himself for a tremendous impact, but this never came; the 911 would glide through without shock, and the performance of the cars in the desert began to come into perspective.

A year later Porsche and Rothmans returned to the Paris-Dakar with a fairly definitive trio of 959s, this being the model's official debut. The kevlar bodywork was in place, including the new headlamp treatment and the swoopy wrap-over rear wing; 16 in (40.5 cm) diameter wheels replaced 15 in (38 cm) diameter and the suspension now featured the 959's upper and lower control arms, with twin Bilstein dampers, though it was not adjustable.

Although the engine was normally-aspirated, and had the 911 Carrera's 3.2-litre capacity, the crankcase was made of magnesium, rather than aluminium, and was 22 lb (10 kg) lighter (production 959s, though, have aluminium crankcases and heads, but magnesium is used for the chain cases, oil pump and filter, fan housing, and manifolds).

The power was only slightly higher, at 230 bhp, but the engine range was more

Three Porsches, now called 959s despite having normally-aspirated engines, were entered in the 1985 Paris-Dakar Raid, but none finished. Ickx and Jochen Maas had accidents, while Metge had an oil line break. The bodywork was lightened and 959 styled, and the definitive four-wheel system was in place.

Above *The 959's education was completed on the 1986 Paris-Dakar Raid, in which René Metge/Dominique Lemoyne were again the winners. Now, on its last event, the 959 had the twin-turbo engine, the electronically controlled centre clutch, and the six-speed gearbox. The suspension, however, was not height adjustable on the move.*

Below *Jacky Ickx and Claude Brasseur finished second on the '86 Paris-Dakar, though twice delayed en route. The Belgian driver, six times winner at Le Mans, was responsible for organizing each of Porsche's forays into the desert.*

effective through use of the new six-speed gearbox, while the four-wheel drive system now featured the five-plate, oil-bathed differential, fully-controlled by the driver. At this stage the electronic control was considered to be unnecessary, and the drivers selected the front/rear torque split by means of a cockpit lever which activated the hydraulic clamping pressure on the plates. The drive could be concentrated at the rear or at the front, or could be split 35:65 or 50:50, which should provide for all possible conditions. The front differential was free-running, but the rear differential had a progressive locking mechanism.

The 1985 event did not turn out nearly so well for Porsche, for both Jacky Ickx and Jochen Mass met with accidents—Ickx hit a boulder at 125 mph (200 km/h), 'exploding' the front of the car—and Metge was the last to retire when an oil line split and the engine was damaged.

In 1986 the Rothmans-Porsche team would contest the Paris-Dakar Rally for the last time, the conclusion of all development work on the main systems prior to series production, but the team wisely decided to have a dress rehearsal and chose the Pharaohs' Rally, in Egypt for a two-car entry. The 'raid', similar to the Paris-Dakar but covering 2,480 miles (4,000 km) of Egyptian desert in ten days, was a good proving ground and the Porsches, for Jacky Ickx/Claude Brasseur and Middle Eastern champion Saeed al Hajri/John Spiller, had virtually the full kit of 959 hardware; the 2.85-litre engine had twin turbo-chargers and developed 400 bhp, the centre differential was controlled by electronic means, with driver over-ride, and the only items 'lacking' were electronically-controlled suspension and anti-lock braking.

Ickx was in trouble on the very first stage; the heat of the turbo-chargers started a blaze in the wiring that ignited the fuel system, and the car was spectacularly destroyed. Al Hajri's car, prepared by Dave Richards Motorsport in England, had its wiring re-routed and gave no problems at all. It won by a handsome margin, beating an unusual car—as a back-up, Kussmaul drove a Mercedes G-Wagen powered by a Porsche 928 engine, and such was the speed of the winner that the Porsche engineer had to drive flat-out to keep in touch, beating a Mitsubishi Pajero into the bargain.

The 1986 Paris Dakar Rally, the last one for Porsche, was even more successful than the 1984 event. René Metge won again, with Dominique Lemoyne, and this time team leader Jacky Ickx finished in second place with Claude Brasseur. Ickx had been delayed twice, first by a rock piercing the front radiator, then by becoming stuck in soft sand, and finished less than two hours behind Metge, with opposition more than three hours behind him. In sixth place was the 959 mounted back-up crew of Roland Kussmaul and Hendrick Unger.

Again I was given the opportunity to drive a Paris-Dakar model 959, this time Ickx's second-place machine. If the 1984 winner had been impressive with 225 bhp, this one was positively explosive with 400 bhp, rocketing from standstill as though the muddy, gravelly surface was high quality asphalt. The six-speed gearbox was surprisingly easy to manage (1-2 spring loaded to the left, 5-6 spring loaded to the right) and offered a wide selection of ratios for various circumstances. . .too many, really, for the non-expert since the 959 would pull

The author prepares to drive Ickx's Paris-Dakar machine, on its return to Germany. Four hundred horsepower, distributed by four wheels, accelerates the car explosively even in mud, and the front-drive techniques takes some mastering. Behind MLC are René Metge (left) and Roland Kussmaul.

strongly from as little as 1,000 rpm in a high gear. For an amateur, third gear was the most suitable for the conditions, taking the car from as little as 30 mph (50 km/h) to as much as 87 mph (140 km/h) without hesitation, the lower gears bouncing the 7,800 rpm rev-limiter almost constantly.

The electronic control box was under the co-driver's seat, and the programme was arranged in four driver-controlled modes, a 'potentiometer' enabling the driver to tune the torque split more exactly. The P1 position, selected by a column lever and indicated, like the others, by a dashboard lamp, sent more torque to the front, but engine power had a greater influence on the ratio. P2 kept more power at the back, but speed had influence on the torque split. C was for constant, the mode used most, and it is here that the driver can use the potentiometer effectively, while T is for traction, locking the centre differential for crawling out of sand traps or mud.

As with the 1984 car, the understeer is quite marked, even though power is not increased at the front wheels once they start to lose grip, and again the steering wheel is very lively in the driver's grip, the front end seeming to 'walk' with plenty of power applied. To ask a layman, even one with rally driving experience, to judge the niceties of a 400 bhp, turbo-charged, four-wheel drive rally car on unknown terrain seemed rather like asking a blind man to judge a Miss World beauty contest! It was clear, though, that the Porsche 959 is an extremely powerful car with extraordinary capabilities in the right hands.

Rally development ceased in January 1986, but the pace of development of the type 961 'evolution model' was stepped up, and the car appeared for the first time, in white, at the Le Mans test day, Roland Kussmaul being the project leader. René Metge and Claude Ballot-Lena drove the 961 in the 24-Hour race.

Mechanical tappets replaced the hydraulic valvegear in the 2.8-litre engine which had been developed, much like the 962C race engines, to a maximum of 680 bhp at 7,800 rpm, maximum torque being 483 lbft (67 mkg) at 5,000 rpm. The car's weight was reduced to 2,530 lb (1,150 kg) (the minimum for the IMSA GTO class), and it was optimistically claimed in the handout material that the maximum speed would be 'almost 400 km/h' (248 mph) which would make it the fastest car on the course. As it turned out the radiator was over-cooled, suggesting too great an intake area, and in the trials the top speed was no higher than 192.6 mph (310 km/h). This was slightly improved to 198 mph (320 km/h) for the race, and the car's best lap time was 3 minutes 47 seconds, some 24 seconds slower than the best Group C lap.

The torque split was set nominally at 40:60 front to rear, with electronic control of the torque setting fine-tuning the ratio constantly, but Kussmaul could not see the 959 winning the race unless it snowed—which seemed a little unlikely in June! Mechanically it was extremely reliable, if unspectacular, and

The competitions evolution of the 959 is numbered 961, and this car made its debut at Le Mans in 1986 when it ran to seventh place overall. The front lid has air exit louvres, the rear wing can be adjusted, and the engine develops up to 680 bhp, but in essence the 961 retains the 959's leading characteristics.

finished in seventh place overall. Such was the distance to the sixth-placed car that it made no difference that a rear tyre had exploded on Sunday morning, necessitating changing a driveshaft (the cv joint disliked being run at a steep angle).

The wheels, as a matter of interest, were 17 in (43 cm) in diameter and 10.25 in (26 cm) wide at the front, 11 in (28 cm) wide at the rear, and the 961 had its second outing at the Daytona 3-Hour race later in the year. The Americans expected rather a lot of this Porsche factory, titanium-expensive wondercar, driven by factory test driver Gunther Steckkonig and Canadian Kees Nierop, and were surprised that after tyre failures during practice, caused by high loads on relatively narrow wheels on the banking, the 961 was run at a conservative speed in the race and finished twenty-forth, 16 laps behind the leaders. Al Holbert asked critics if any other car in the GTO class could win the Paris-Dakar Rally, but not many had even heard of it. Holbert confirmed that the US delivered price was $340,000, then equivalent to DM650,000, but there were no takers.

Development of the 961 continued in 1987, and a 961 was entered for Le Mans in Rothmans colours for Claude Haldi/René Metge/Kees Nierop. This outing was not a great success as the rear driveshaft constant velocity joints failed, the clutch was difficult to operate and the gears hard to select. Due to these problems Nierop spun the car and damaged it on Sunday morning, forcing retirement.

Track driving the 959

It is one experience to drive a pair of noisy, beaten-up rally cars through mud, water and gravel, but quite another to drive a completely-refined, production prototype 959 model on the Nürburgring racing circuit. That, too, was my privilege in 1986, much more realistic too since there was no compulsion to drive quickly, making it possible to judge just how effective this car might be on public highways.

The smell of leather and the air of luxury is the first impression on climbing in, and the controls are familiar, though certainly more numerous and complex than in a 911 Turbo. Turning the key brings life to the engine which ticks over easily at 700 rpm, and blipping the throttle creates a noise that owes more to a 962 racing car than a normal Turbo, though well muffled.

It takes a couple of laps to build up confidence, and to learn that the 959 is no animal. The very idea of loading another 220 lb (100 kg) of weight to the already tail-heavy Turbo is inhibiting, yet the 959 feels extremely well-balanced and anything but wayward, and that is a surprise. As speed builds up the car displays understeer, not oversteer, a characteristic that has been deliberately applied.

The acceleration seems ferocious at first but at consistently high speeds on a wide open race track the 959 is impressive, but not neck-snapping, and the time even came on the main straight when I noted the hole in the curve, the pause in acceleration between 4,000 rpm, the top of the primary turbo's curve, and 4,500 rpm when the secondary turbo comes in strongly. The brakes were a revelation, the pedal firm but responsive, the 962-type discs (12.7 in (324 mm) in diameter at the front) seeming to have unlimited capacity to pull the car down from 124 mph (200 km/h) with certainty. Anti-lock brake systems have been criticized for increasing the distance of retardation on dry roads, but Porsche's own tests show that the Wabco system produces 1.2g deceleration from 100 km/h and 1.27g deceleration from 300 km/h, amazing figures.

There comes a moment when braking is left almost too late at the end of the main straight, and the pedal is hit very hard. Not only do the wheels not lock up, but there is no 'pulsing' that a Bosch system would promote in the pedal. And then, *in extremis*, the 959 allows the driver to do something unthinkable in a Turbo, and turn-in with the brakes still applied! There is just a gentle lurch in the rear suspension and the car settles in to the corner, where a Turbo would be spinning like a top.

Half an hour on the track is enough for most people, all that was allowed by Porsche. The exertion of cornering and of constantly moving through most of the six gears takes its toll on arm muscles but the car still feels fresh and the brakes as firm as ever. Then Gunther Steckkonig, chief test driver— reputed to be the fastest man in a 959—took over and gave the car a completely new dimension, cornering so much quicker that he was always one gear higher.

On a dry, high-grip surface it had made little difference in which driving mode the torque-split was set, and there had been no particular sensation, other than mild understeer in slow turns, felt through the superb steering system. Steckkonig, though, would tackle the corners aggressively, forcing the tail to slide on entry and bringing it back into line with full throttle applications, and with the front wheels sliding too, in a full-blooded drift, it was possible to see feed-back in the steering wheel. Now the 959 would understeer strongly, and would need a throttle lift to make it point the right way, though at speeds far in excess of any that might be achieved on normal roads.

This is the Porsche 959, a road car faster than any other and, treated with respect, safer than any other. Its capabilities are clearly greater than those of most of the customers who have bought them, and it is without doubt a technological showcase. The future of the 911 range is full of the most fascinating possibilities, which is the message that Porsche spells out with the 959.

Appendix

Porsche Road Car Specifications—1974 to 1987

Year	Model	Cylinders	Compression ratio
1974-77	911 2.7	6	8.5
1975-77	911 Carrera	6	8.5
1975-77	911 Turbo	6	6.5
1975-85	924	4	9.3
1977-79	928	8	8.5
1978-79	911 SC	6	8.5
1978-82	911 Turbo 3.3	6	7.0
1978-80	924 Turbo	4	7.5
1979-82	928S	8	10.0
1979-82	928	8	10.0
1980	924 Carrera GT	4	8.5
1980-81	911 SC	6	8.6
1981-83	911 SC	6	9.8
1981-83	924 Turbo	4	8.5
1981-	944	4	10.6
1982-	911 Turbo	6	7.0
1983-	911 Carrera	6	10.3
1983-86	928S	8	10.4
1985-	944 Turbo	4	8.0
1985-	924S	4	9.7
1985-86	928S (USA)	8	10.0
1986-	928S-4	8	10.0
1986-	944S	4	10.0
1987	959	6	8.3

Porsche Competitions Car Specifications—1974 to 1987

Year	Model	Cylinders	Turbo	Valves per cylinder	Compression ratio
1974	911 Carrera Turbo	6	1	2	6.5
1976	934 Gp 4	6	1	2	6.5
	935 Gp 5	6	1	2	6.5
	936 Gp 6	6	1	2	6.5
1977	935/77	6	2	2	6.5
	935/2.0	6	1	2	6.5
	936/77	6	2	2	6.5
1978	935/78	6	2	4	7.0
	935/3.1	6	2	2	7.0
	936/78	6	2	4	7.0
1980	935 (IMSA)	6	2	2	7.0
	P6B Indy	6	1	4	9.0
	924 GTP	4	1	2	6.8
1981	936/81	6	2	4	7.0
	924 GTR	4	1	2	7.0
	944 GTP	4	1	4	7.0
1982	956	6	2	4	7.0
1983	956	6	2	4	8.0
1984	962 IMSA	6	1	2	6.5
	911 SC RS	6	—	2	10.3
1985	962C	6	2	4	9.0
1986	962C	6	2	4	9.0
	961	6	2	4	9.0
1987	2708 Indy	8	1	4	11.0

Bore (mm) × stroke, mm	Capacity cc	Power (bhp @ rpm)	Torque (mkg) @ rpm	Length (cm)	Width (cm)	Wheelbase (cm)	Weight (kg)
90 × 70.4	2,687	175 @ 5,800	24 @ 4,000	429.1	161	227.1	1,075
95 × 70.4	2,994	200 @ 6,000	26 @ 4,200	429.1	166.1	227.1	1,120
95 × 70.4	2,994	260 @ 5,500	35 @ 4,000	429.1	177.8	227.1	1,240
86.5 × 84.4	1,984	125 @ 5,800	16.8 @ 3,500	421.3	167.6	240	1,080
95 × 78.9	4,474	240 @ 5,500	35.6 @ 3,600	444.7	183.6	250	1,490
95 × 70.4	2,994	180 @ 5,500	27 @ 4,200	429.1	166.1	227.1	1,160
97 × 74.4	3,299	300 @ 5,500	42 @ 4,000	429.1	177.8	227.1	1,300
86.5 × 84.4	1,984	170 @ 5,800	25 @ 3,500	421.3	167.6	240	1,180
97 × 78.9	4,664	300 @ 5,900	39 @ 4,500	446.2	183.6	250	1,550
95 × 78.9	4,474	240 @ 5,250	39 @ 3,600	444.7	183.6	250	1,520
86.5 × 84.4	1,984	210 @ 6,000	28.5 @ 3,500	432	172.7	240	1,180
95 × 70.4	2,994	188 @ 5,500	27 @ 4,200	429.1	166.1	227.1	1,160
95 × 70.4	2,994	204 @ 5,900	27 @ 4,300	429.1	166.1	227.1	1,160
86.5 × 84.4	1,984	177 @ 5,500	25.5 @ 3,500	421.3	167.6	240	1,180
100 × 78.9	2,479	163 @ 5,800	20.9 @ 3,000	421.3	173.5	240	1,180
97 × 74.4	3,299	300 @ 5,500	44 @ 4,000	429.1	177.8	227.1	1,300
95 × 74.4	3,164	231 @ 5,900	29 @ 4,800	429.1	166.1	227.1	1,160
97 × 78.9	4,664	310 @ 5,900	40.8 @ 4,100	446.2	183.6	250	1,550
100 × 78.9	2,479	220 @ 5,800	33.6 @ 3,500	423	173.5	240	1,350
100 × 78.9	2,479	150 @ 5,800	19.4 @ 3,000	421.3	173.5	240	1,210
100 × 78.9	4,957	288 @ 5,750	41.7 @ 2,700	446.2	183.6	250	1,550
100 × 78.9	4,957	320 @ 6,000	43.9 @ 3,000	446.2	183.6	250	1,580
100 × 78.9	2,479	190 @ 6,000	23.4 @ 4,300	423	173.5	250	1,280
95 × 67	2.857	450 @ 6,500	51 @ 5,500	426	184	227.1	1,450

Bore (mm) × stroke (mm)	Capacity (cc)	Power (bhp @ rpm)	Torque (mkg) @ rpm	Length (cm)	Width (cm)	Wheelbase (cm)	Weight (kg)
83 × 66	2,142	500 @ 7,600	56 @ 5,400	423.5	202	227.1	825
95 × 70.4	2,994	485 @ 7,000	60 @ 5,400	420	187	227.1	1,120
92.8 × 70.4	2,856	590 @ 7,900	60 @ 5,400	468	200	227.1	970
83 × 66	2,142	520 @ 8,000	48 @ 6,000	420	198	240	720
92.8 × 70.4	2,856	630 @ 8,000	60 @ 5,400	468	200	227.1	970
71 × 60	1,425	370 @ 8,000	n/a	468	196	227.1	720
83× 66	2,142	540 @ 8,000	50 @ 6,000	470	192	240	750
95.7 × 74.4	3,211	750 @ 8,200	85 @ 6,500	478	199	227.9	1,025
97 × 70.4	3,124	680 @ 8,000	72 @ 5,600	468	200	227.1	1,025
87 × 60.4	2,140	580 @ 8,500	53 @ 6,000	474	192	243	800
95 × 74.4	3,164	720 @ 8,000	75 @ 5,500	468	200	227.1	1,025
92.8 × 66	2,650	630 @ 9,000	57 @ 6,400	455	206	n/a	680
86.5 × 84.4	1,984	320 @ 7,000	39 @ 4,500	420	185	240	930
92.8 × 66	2,650	620 @ 8,000	62 @ 6,200	474	192	243	825
86.5 × 84.4	1,984	375 @ 6,400	41 @ 5,600	424	185	240	945
100 × 78.9	2,479	420 @ 6,800	n/a	424	187	240	950
92.8 × 66	2,650	620 @ 8,000	62 @ 5,400	480	200	265	850
92.8 × 66	2,650	630 @ 8,000	64 @ 5,400	480	200	265	850
92.8 × 70.4	2,856	650 @ 8,000	65 @ 5,400	480	199	279.5	885
95 × 70.4	2,994	255 @ 7,000	26 @ 6,500	429	175	227.1	960
92.8 × 70.4	2,856	650 @ 8,200	70 @ 5,000	477	199	279.5	870
95 × 70.4	2,994	650 @ 8,200	72 @ 5,000	477	199	279.5	870
95 × 67	2,857	680 @ 7,800	67 @ 5,000	438	189	231	1,150
88.2 × 54.2	2,649	740 @ 11,200	47 @ 8,500	466	201	280	703

Index